THE IS TANKS

IS-1, IS-2, IS-3

MIKHAIL BARYATINSKIY

Ian Allan

PUBLISHING

First published 2006

ISBN (10) 0 7110 3162 2
ISBN (13) 978 0 7110 3162 3

Published by Ian Allan Publishing

an imprint of Ian Allan Publishing Ltd,
Hersham, Surrey KT12 4RG.
Printed by Ian Allan Printing Ltd, Hersham,
Surrey KT12 4RG.

Code: 0604/B2

An IS-2 of the 7th Guards Heavy Tank Brigade near the Brandenburg Gate,
Berlin, May 1945. The wide white stripes only visible on turret sides – also
painted on turret top rather than tank served for friend-or-foe identification
by Russian and Allied pilots.

Design concept and layout by Polygon Press
Ltd. (Moscow, Russia).
Drawings by Mikhail Dmitriyev.
Line drawings by Mikhail Dmitriyev
and Mikhail Baryatinskiy.

This book is illustrated with photos from the
collections of M. Baryatinskiy, M. Kolomiets,
A. Aksyonov, A. Shelyakin, S. Balakin,
Ya. Manguskiy.

Contents

INTRODUCTION

In the early years of World War 2, the Soviet Union and Nazi Germany were the two countries running a substantial fleet of heavy tanks – an often contested proposition because the German Pz.IVs, officially classified as heavy, were closer to medium in terms of performance. The gap between Soviet KVs and the rest of the world had seemed unbridgeable until the end of 1942 when the German Tiger caught up. This competition between the Soviets and the Nazis shaped the heavy armour agenda until the end of the war. The Anglo-American Allies did little in this department, with the US M26 being the only design that could count as a genuine heavy tank.

Iosef Stalin, or IS, the new Soviet heavy tank, was fielded in 1943 and later repeatedly upgraded. It was a product of vast if bitter experience – the IS's predecessor KV (Kliment Voroshilov), operational in 1940-1944, though superior to all 1941 peers in terms of firepower, manoeuvrability, and armour protection (but not operational reliability) was severely underestimated and misplaced tactically. In 1941-1942 Soviet armour brigades were a wild mix of light, medium, and heavy tanks, which nullified all the KV's advantages. Ironically, the late 1942 KV version, reliable enough and tactically well organized into "breakthrough" regiments, was already inferior to the Tiger. What was even worse, the KV was hardly upgradable as heavier armament and protection would severely undermine manoeuvrability.

The Soviet military demanded a conceptually new heavy tank that would combine firepower and protection with a low silhouette and relatively light weight, crucial to manoeuvrability and survivability. Nearly three years of war were particularly helpful in refining these requirements specifications.

The most brilliant IS advantages stemmed from the progressive Russian vision of the role of heavy tanks on the battlefield. While the Nazis saw heavy tanks primarily as an antitank asset, their Russian peers were designed for a diverse range of combat missions. The IS-2 with the D-25T gun was absolute World War 2 champion in terms of high-explosive/fragmentation firepower, which contributed greatly to Soviet successes against the heavily defended Königsberg and Berlin.

Encouraged by the IS-2, the Soviet military pushed for even thicker armour and innovative body and turret silhouettes that gave the new IS-3 almost absolute protection against all contemporary ordnance. However, the tank was too heavy to be reliable, and was effectively barred from military exercises in the 1950s-60s, becoming largely a November-7-parade-style demonstration of Soviet military power.

IS-1 and IS-2

ORIGINS

The IS-2 heavy tank dates back to the KV-1 and KV-13 tanks. The former is known pretty well while information on the latter could until recently only have been gained from a couple of publications dedicated to the SKB-2 design bureau of the Kirovsky plant. Therefore, greater light should be shed on the KV-13.

The KV-13 (factory designation – Object 233) was the first independently designed product of the Experimental Tank Plant established in March 1942 on the premises of the SKB-2 design bureau in Chelyabinsk. The project's chief designer was N. V. Tseits who had been released

from the gulag. The KV-13 development relied on the concept of a versatile tank whose weight would equal that of the medium tank while the armour protection would be as good as that of the heavy tank. The project featured a heavy use of armoured casting. Both the turret and the main elements of the hull, the bow, turret compartment sides and roof and rear section, were cast. This allowed a reduction in unusable internal space, differentiation of the armour protection and, as a result, a reduction in armour plating. The latter consideration was rather important, all the more so in the light of the 23 February 1942 order issued by the State Defence Committee to save rolled armour as much as possible.

A KV-13 tank in the yard of the Experimental Tank Plant in Chelyabinsk, 1942.

A prototype of the IS-1 (in-house product code 'Object 233') at Plant No. 100 in Chelyabinsk, in the spring of 1943.

The first vehicle was designed and made very quickly, and its factory trials started in May 1942. The tank weighed 31.7 tonnes and mounted the 76-mm ZIS-5 main gun and DT coaxial machine-gun. The glacis plate was 120 mm thick, with the front armour of the turret measuring 85 mm. The V-2K engine featured a maximum horsepower of 600 hp and produced a maximum speed of 55 km/h. The running gear, including the tracks, was borrowed from the T-34 and the roadwheels from the KV. The KV-13 was fitted with a U-shaped radiator similar to that equipping the T-50 light tank (the Kirovsky plant's variant). This allowed the engine compartment to be packed tighter and the boosted efficiency of the airflow driven by the fan. An ingenious nine-speed gearbox with a triple auxiliary gearbox was coaxial to the planetary final drives.

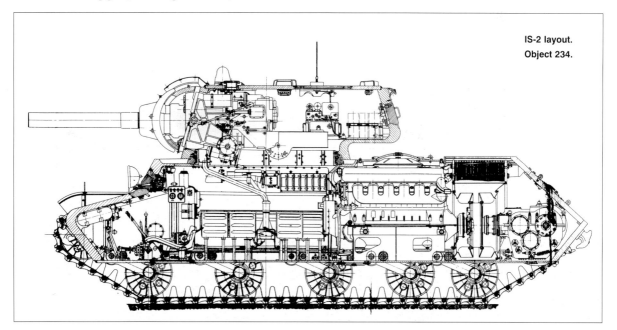

IS-2 layout. Object 234.

The prototype of the IS-2 (Object 234) at Plant No. 100, Chelyabinsk, in the spring of 1943.

The trials of the first KV-13 tank highlighted several deficiencies, such as problems with the gearbox's acceleration characteristics, disintegration of roadwheels and track links, throwing of tracks while turning, etc. N. V. Tseits passed away when the trials were in full swing and was succeeded by N. F. Shashmurin. Shashmurin had the KV-13 fitted with the gearbox and running gear elements developed for the KV-1S tank. However, the tank failed its tests in spite of the efforts made, which caused the Red Army inter-

est in the tank to cool considerably. Still, the Experimental Tank Plant launched assembly, albeit sluggish, of two new versions of the KV-13 in December 1942.

To fit the new versions, only the hull, torsion-bar suspension and five-roadwheel running gear were borrowed from the initial version. Their turrets and many other units had to be designed from scratch. Their transmission featured two-stage planetary steering gears developed by A. I. Blagonravov. The cooling system was improved, and the drive train comprised only units borrowed from the KV-1S, with the tracks having been made lighter by using only odd lug-less track links.

The speed of manufacturing the tanks was stepped up by the fact that the advanced Tiger heavy tank was introduced by the Germans on the Eastern Front between autumn 1942 and winter 1943.

On 24 February 1943, the State Defence Committee ordered the Chelyabinsk-based Kirovsky plant and Plant 100 of the People's Commissariat for Heavy Industry (the then new designation of the Experimental Tank Plant) to make and submit for official testing two prototypes of the Iosef Stalin tank, the IS. The last variants of the KV-13 were used as the initial examples. One, armed with the 76-mm ZIS-5 gun, was designated as IS-1 (in-house designation Object 233) and the other, mounting the 122-mm U-11 howitzer in the turret of the KV-9 heavy tank, was dubbed IS-2 (Object 234).

The 'Object 237' (IS No. 1) heavy tank in the yard of Plant No. 100, Chelyabinsk, July 1943.

Both vehicles were tested from 22 March to 19 April 1943, with the trials being a success. The acceptance committee admitted that, compared with the KV-1S, the two IS prototypes featured tighter layouts, lower weight, better armour protection and higher speed, with the IS-1's armament being similar to and the IS-2's being more formidable than that of the KV-1S. However, there were serious deficiencies, too, featured mostly by the powerpack and running gear. On soft ground the tanks encountered tractive resistance caused by the track links flexing between the roadwheels. Tractive resistance proved to be higher than that of the KV-1S. The acceptance committee recommended that the number of roadwheels should be increased.

'Object 237' fording a river during manufacturer's tests, July 1943.

Object 237 (IS-2) passing a testing programme. Chelyabinsk, summer 1943.

'Object 238' – a production KV-1S armed with an 85-mm S-18 prototype cannon.

Concurrently with the trials conducted by the Kirovsky plant, preparations for full-rate production of the advanced tanks were in full swing at Plant 100 and its main subcontractors – UZTM and Plant 200. However, the preparations had to be adjusted significantly. In early April, solid intelligence was obtained on the Tiger's armour protection, and the State Defence Committee ordered the People's Commissariat for Armament as early as 15 April to develop formidable main guns to enable Soviet tanks to kill their advanced hostile rivals.

In late April, the only captured Tiger was shot up by various artillery pieces at the proving ground of the Research Institute of Armoured Materiel (Russian acronym – NIIBT) in Kubinka (Moscow Region). It was discovered that the 85-mm 52-K anti-aircraft gun, dating back to 1939, proved to be the most effective means against the Tiger, punching through its 100-mm armour at a range of up to 1,000 m. Dated 5 May 1943, the State Defence Committee's resolution On Enhancing Tank and Self-Propelled Gun Armament prompted the design bureaux to focus on the gun's ballistic characteristics. The resolution ordered the Central Artillery Design Bureau (Russian acronym – TsAKB), led by V. G. Grabin, and the design bureau of the People's Commissariat for Armament's Plant 9, led by Chief Designer F. F. Petrov, to develop 85-mm guns featuring the ballistic characteristics of the 52-K AA gun on two KV-1S tanks and two IS prototypes.

In early June, the four main guns – two S-31s from TsAKB and two D-5Ts from Plant 9 – were completed. The S-31 was developed by mating the 85-mm tube with the cradle of the production 76-mm ZIS-5 tank gun, which would make production far easier. The D-5T was a derivative of the D-5S developed to fit the SU-85 self-propelled gun (SPG). The D-5T featured low weight and a short length of recoil.

As early as the conceptual design stage of the 85-mm gun-fitted IS tank development, it became clear that a turret ring diameter of 1,535 mm made it impossible for the vehicle to mount such a weapon without degrading the crew's efficiency sharply. The designers therefore opted to increase the turret ring diameter to 1,800-mm by extending the fighting compartment and, hence, the tank's length by 420 mm.

Since the length of the hull between the second and third roadwheels now stretched too far, a sixth roadwheel had to be added on each side. A new turret was cast by Plant 200 to fit the larger-diameter turret ring. The modifications drove the tank's weight up to 44 tonnes, reduced its specific horsepower and hampered its dynamics. It was the price to pay for the more lethal main armament. The tank, mounting the 85-mm main gun, was designated as Object 237. Two IS prototypes were completed in early July 1943, fitted with the S-31 and D-5T guns respectively.

While running the Object 237 development programme, the Kirovsky plant also came up with two preliminary designs to fit the 85-mm gun to the KV-1S tank. One variant, Object 238, was in essence a production KV-1S mounting the S-31 main gun in the original turret, and the other, Object 239, included the D-5T-equipped turret of Object 237.

July 1943 saw the comparative testing of all four tanks. As a result, the D-5T gun and Objects 237 and 239 were chosen, with the tanks being designated as IS-85 and KV-85 respectively. Object 238 was rejected due to its very cramped fighting compartment preventing the crew from operating efficiently.

The KV-85 and IS-85 arrived at NIIBT's proving ground in Kubinka on 31 July for official trials with 28 specialists in tow led by Plant 100's Chief Engineer N. M. Sinev. The tests, which were conducted by an acceptance committee chaired by Maj.-Gen. S. A. Afonin, chief of the Technical Department of the Main Armoured Directorate of the Red Army, began at the Gorokhovetsky gunnery range on 2 August. The tests being a success, the acceptance committee sanctioned the introduction of both tanks.

Then, the vehicles were ferried to the premises of the evacuated Plant 37 at the Cherkizovo railway station in the Moscow Region (now a district of Moscow). On 8 August, a convoy of the prototypes rolled down Moscow's streets to the Kremlin where they were shown to Stalin, Molotov, Voroshilov, Beria, Fedorenko, Malyshev, etc. Before the leaders examined the tanks, their crews were ordered away, save for the drivers, and replaced with NKVD security service officers.

On 4 September 1943, the State Defence Committee ordered the IS-85 heavy tank into the Red Army's inventory. The same order tasked Plant 100 with designing, making and testing an IS tank with a 122-mm gun in conjunction with the Main Armoured Directorate's Technical Department by 15 October 1943 and designing, making and testing its derivative, the IS-152 self-propelled gun.

As implied above, the IS-2 tank mounting the 122-mm gun and the ISU-152 SPG were not shown to Stalin at the time in spite of numerous publications to the contrary. IS-2 with the D-5T and the SU-152 (KV-14) self-propelled gun and an improved fighting compartment ventilating system must have been mistaken for the IS-2.

Mention should be made that the acceptance committee came up with a range of proposals to improve the IS tank's design, with some of them obviously influenced by foreign experiences. The latter included proposals to develop and test a hydraulic traversing mechanism similar to that on the US-made M4A2 tank and a turreted antiaircraft machinegun mounted on the hatch of the cupola, to fit the turret with a 50-mm breech-loaded mortar for self-defence and launching signal flares, and to design a cradle to fit 85-mm, 100-mm, 122-mm and 152-mm main guns.

The 'Object 239' experimental tank after live firing trials. Chelyabinsk, July 1943.

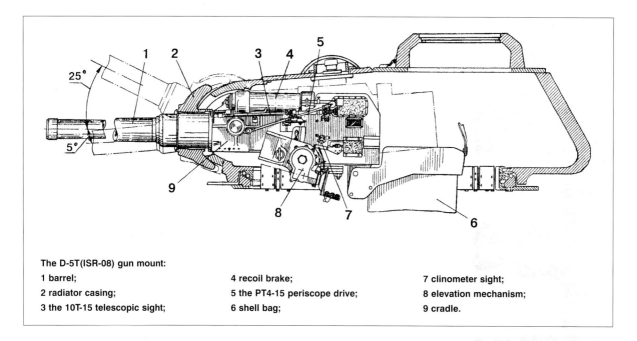

The D-5T(ISR-08) gun mount:

1 barrel;	4 recoil brake;	7 clinometer sight;
2 radiator casing;	5 the PT4-15 periscope drive;	8 elevation mechanism;
3 the 10T-15 telescopic sight;	6 shell bag;	9 cradle.

Zh. Ya. Kotin, director and chief designer of Plant 100, was the one who suggested the IS should be up-gunned. In early 1943 while analysing the outcome of the Battle of Kursk, he noticed that the 122-mm A-19 gun vintage 1931/1937, operated at the corps level, proved to be the most lethal of all artillery systems used against Tigers. His opinion was shared by Plant 9 designers who developed a prototype of the D-2 heavy antitank gun by fitting the A-19's tube to the undercarriage of the 122-mm D-30 divisional howitzer. This mighty weapon was supposed to be used primarily against the enemy's heavy armour. However, since its barrel was mounted on the cradle and undercarriage of the M-30 and the resulting weapon passed its tests, it became feasible to fit the A-19's tube to the heavy tank through the use of the circular cradle, recoil mechanisms and elevation gear of the 122-mm U-11 prototype tank howitzer, as was done in developing the 85-mm D-5T and D-5S guns. In fact, it was feasible only by reducing the barrel's length by 245 mm and introducing a muzzle brake to the design.

IS-1, 1st Guards Heavy Tank Breakthrough Regiment, 11th Guards Tank Corps. Ukraine, March 1944.

Having been provided with relevant documentation by Plant 100, Plant 9's design bureau was quick to complete the conceptual design of the configuration comprising the A-19 gun in the IS-85's turret. Zh. Ya. Kotin took the draft to Moscow. The people's commissar for armour industry, V. A. Malyshev, liked it and Stalin approved it. The IS tank fitted with the 122-mm gun entered the inventory of the Red Army under the State Defence Committee resolution dated 31 October 1943. Plant 9 was tasked with making the tank version of the screw-type breechblock A-19 gun by 11 November 1943 and submitting it for trials by 27 November 1943. At the same time, the gun was to be fitted with a wedge-type breechblock and enter production in 1944. Permission also was granted to make 100-mm gun prototypes to fit the IS tank.

The first example of the tank-mounted A-19 gun was made on 12 November through mating the D-5T's cradle with the D-2's barrel from an M-30, with its lead-in section machined additionally to match the cradle's diameter. The T-shaped muzzle brake was borrowed from the D-2 as well.

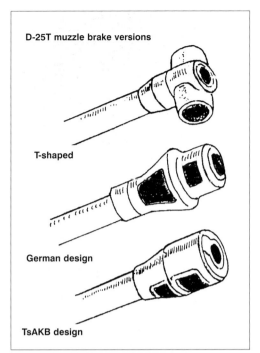

D-25T muzzle brake versions

T-shaped

German design

TsAKB design

Experimental Object 240, Chelyabinsk, September, 1943. This tank's gun ends with a T-shaped muzzle brake.

Driver's compartment:
1 – driver's seat; 2 – left fuel tank; 3 – right fuel tank; 4 – manual auxiliary fuel pump; 5 – manual fuel feeding lever; 6 – fuel distribution valve; 7 – overflow tank; 8 – steering levers; 9 – compressed air bottles; 10 – accelerator pedal; 11 – master clutch pedal; 12 – gear lever; 13 – auxiliary gearbox lever; 14 – instrument panel; 15 – engine revolution indicator; 16 – driver's electric panel; 17 – prism sights (periscopes); 18 – driver's visor vision block; 19 – lock for driver's visor; 20 – buzzer button; 21 – trigger for fixed machine gun; 22 – intratank communication headset; 23 – speed indicator.

Early IS-2 (1944) with notable cast front with "broken" nose and driver's direct vision armoured visor. The turret features the marrow gun mantlet and an armoured cover for the commander's cupola.

One of the last IS-2s made in 1944. The new turret with a wider gun mantlet, and an MK-15 periscope instead of the PT4-17, is fitted to the original type of hull with the "broken" nose.

The official trials of the IS-122 (Object 240) tank were quick and, essentially, a success. Then, the tank was driven to a testing ground in the Moscow Region where its 122-mm gun fired a shot at an empty Panther tank at 1,500 m range, with Klim Voroshilov observing the firing. Having punched through the side of the turret that was turned right, the projectile hit the opposite side's armour plate, tore it off and threw it several metres. During the trials, the A-19's T-shaped muzzle brake blew up, with Voroshilov surviving by the skin of his teeth. The muzzle brake had to be replaced with the German twin-chamber design.

The first production IS-85s were made in October 1943, with the first IS-122s in December. Concurrent with making IS tanks, the Kirovsky plant had continued to build KV-85s until the end of 1943. The last 40 IS-85s rolled out of the assembly shop in January 1944, with the plant then switching to making only IS-122s in growing numbers. Plant 9 started manufacturing screw-breech D-25 guns instead of D-5Ts. The first 10 guns were completed in November 1943, with their total number standing at 147.

In late 1943, Plant 9 developed a semiautomatic drop-breech to fit the D-25 gun. The first example of the upgraded gun as well as the advanced TSh-17 sight had been mounted on the Object 240 prototype by 6 February. Plant 69 of the People's Commissariat for Armament had been developing the TSh-17 hinged telescopic sight since September 1943 in line with the task set by People's Commissar for Armament

IS-1 and IS-2 Heavy Tank Production

	IS-1	IS-2
1943		
October	2	–
November	25	–
December	40	35
Total:	**67**	**35**
1944		
January	40	35
February	–	75
March	–	100
April	–	150
May	–	175
June	–	200
July	–	225
August	–	250
September	–	250
October	–	250
November	–	250
December	–	250
Total:	**40**	**2,210**
1945		
until 9 May	–	997
after 9 May	–	1,150
Total:	**–**	**2,147**
Total:	**107**	**4,392**

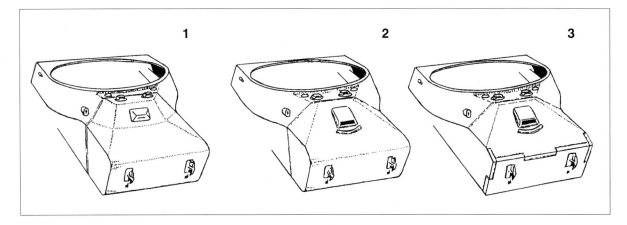

1   **2**   **3**

IS-2 nose versions:
1 – Parent (cast "broken");
2 – cast with "streamlined" nose, producer ChKZ;
3 – welded with "streamlined" nose, producer UZTM.

D. F. Ustinov – "launch the full-rate production of sights similar to the German ones". The D-25 drop-breech gun underwent its factory and official trials in February and March 1944, having fired 819 shots. The acceptance committee concluded that the weapon passed the tests and was easier to operate than the screw-type breech-block one. Introduction of the wedge-type breechblock allowed a slight increase in the rate of fire from 1-1.5 rd/min. to 1.5-2 rd/min. In March 1944, this D-25 version entered full-scale production, with its German-type muzzle brake replaced with a more efficient design from TsAKB. From then on, the IS-85 was re-designated as IS-1 and IS-122 as IS-2, though the four designations were used indiscriminately in documents at the time. Mention should be made that early-series IS-122 tanks were often called KV-122 in reports coming from the front.

DESCRIPTION

The IS tank had a classic configuration with the engine compartment in the rear. The driving compartment was in the front part of the hull. It housed the driver's seat, two fuel tanks, driver's controls, instruments, two air bottles, central fuel valve, manual fuel pump, hull machinegun trigger button and some of the spares, tools and accessories. There was an emergency escape hatch in the floor behind the driver's seat.

The fighting compartment was situated behind the driving compartment in the middle of the hull. It cotained the loader's, gunner's and commander's seats, hull machinegun, the bulk of the ammunition load, batteries, heaters, turret collector ring box and part of the spares, tools and accessories. Engine and gearbox control rods ran on the floor of this compartment.

The first operational IS-2 with a cast "streamlined" nose.

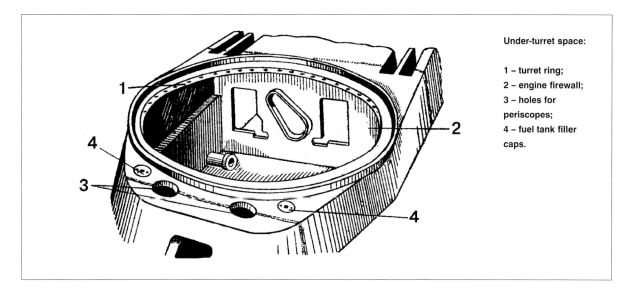

Under-turret space:

1 – turret ring;
2 – engine firewall;
3 – holes for periscopes;
4 – fuel tank filler caps.

The turret above the fighting compartment housed the main gun and two machineguns, sights and observation devices, part of the ammunition load, a radio, turret traversing mechanisms, fighting compartment ventilator and part of the spares, tools and accessories.

The engine compartment was behind the fighting one, separated by a firewall. The engine was mounted on brackets in the centre. There were fuel and oil tanks on the right and left sides of it respectively. There were oil coolers under them, with 'multicyclone' air filters on both sides at the front of the compartment.

The transmission compartment was at the very rear of the hull. It housed the engine clutch, centrifugal fan, gearbox, planetary steering gears and final drives.

Water radiators were installed in the screen between the engine and transmission compartments above the radiator fan.

The hull was a rigid welded armour box made of cast and rolled armour. The hull's cast parts were the bow and turret fighting compartment sides and roof. The rolled parts were the hull bottom, sides, rear and top of the engine deck.

The glacis plate included the driver's direct vision port with armoured cover. The front part of the hull's roof had two periscopes to watch terrain with the port closed. Access to the driving compartment was via the turret hatches only.

The shot deflector ring attached to the lower turret ring was welded to the turret pedestal. The recessed under-turret belt made the turret's jamming impossible.

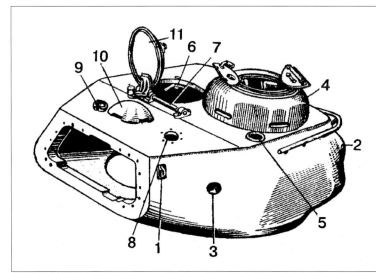

Turret:

1 – lifting hooks;
2 – rear machinegun mounting bulge;
3 – small arms firing port;
4 – commander's cupola;
5 – radio antenna plug;
6 – loader's hatch lock;
7 – torsion bar spring;
8 – hole for PT4-15 or PT4-17 periscope or MK-IV sight;
9 – MK-IV sight hole;
10 – ventilator armoured cover;
11 – loader's hatch.

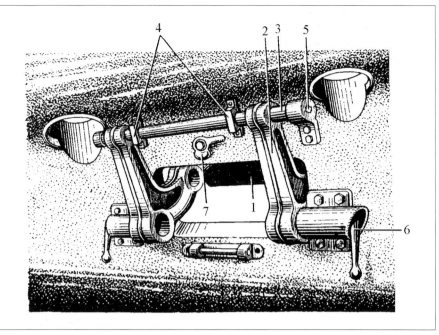

Driver's hatch protection:

1 – armoured port cover;
2 – crank lever;
3 - tube;
4 - brackets;
5 - torsion bar spring;
6 - lock;
7 - lever.

The rear hull plate was in three sections – upper, middle and lower. The middle plate was hinged, the upper one was detachable and the lower one was welded to the hull sides and bottom.

The bow was modified in May 1944, with the plug-type driver's vision port cover replaced by prismatic-glass vision slit.

The streamlined-shape turret was cast. Its front had an embrasure covered by an elevating mantlet with three firing ports for the main gun, coaxial machinegun and telescopic sight. There was a boss in the rear of the turret, housing a hinged rear machinegun. There were firing ports for personal weapons, protected by armoured covers on the sides of the turret.

Engine compartment cover.

A cupola with an entrance hatch and six viewing slits was welded to the turret roof. There was a hatch to the right of the cupola for the crew to get in and out of the vehicle.

The turret was traversed by an electric motor or manually operated. The electric drive ensured a maximum traversing speed of 2.4 rotations per minute.

The IS-1 mounted the 85-mm 48.8-calibre (some sources mention 52 calibres) D-5T (or D-5-T85) gun that weighed 1,530 kg. Elevation ranged from –5 deg. to +25 deg. The weapon was fitted with the drop-breech and cam-plate semi-automatics, as well as hydraulic recoil brake and hydropneumatic recuperator, both situated above the tube, with the recuperator on the right and the recoil brake on the left of it.

The gun was fired by means of an electric trigger, the button of which was on the elevation gear's hand-wheel.

Late 1944 IS-2 at the research site, Kubinka, Moscow Region.

Engine compartment cover.

The 85-mm D-5T gun before installation.

Round	O-365	BR-365	OF-471	BR-471
Calibre, mm	85	85	122	122
Weight, kg	.	9.2	25	25
Muzzle velocity, m/s	785	792	781	781

The tank mounted three 7.62-mm DT machine-guns, of which two were in the turret and one was the hull machinegun. One of the machineguns in the turret was coaxial and the other was mounted in the machinegun ball mount in the turret rear armour plate. The hull machinegun was fixed rigidly in parallel with the hull's longitudinal axis within a tube welded into the armour plate.

To direct-fire the D-5T gun and coaxial machinegun, the 10T-15 telescopic sight and PT4-15 periscope sight were used. To deliver plunging fire, the gun was fitted with the gun sight elevation level. The rear machinegun could be fitted with the PU sniper optical sight.

The IS-1's ammunition load comprised 59 main gun rounds (53-UO-365 fixed rounds with fragmentation projectiles and 53-UBR-365 unitary rounds with armour-piercing/tracer projectiles) and 2,520 rounds of ammunition for the machineguns.

The rounds were stowed in the turret, behind the front fuel tanks in the hull, on the fight compartment sides and in ammo boxes on the floor of the fighting compartment.

The IS-2 mounted the 122-mm 48-calibre D-25T gun with a muzzle brake. It weighed 2,420 kg. The maximum recoil length was 570 mm, elevation ranged from –3 deg. to +20 deg.

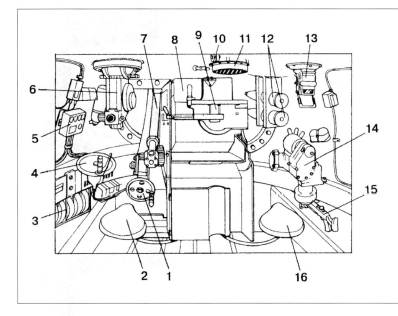

Early IS-2 turret front from inside:

1 – gun elevation gear;
2 – gunner's seat;
3 – machine-gun ammunition stowage;
4 – manual turret rotation mechanism;
5 – turret intercom panel;
6 – the PT4-17 periscope;
7 – the 10T-17 telescope;
8 – breech end of the gun;
9 – interrupted screw breechblock;
10 – bracket securing the gun in the travelling position;
11 – fighting compartment ventilator;
12 – 122-mm ammunition;
13 – the MK-IV sight;
14 – turret traverse motor;
15 – DT coaxial machinegun;
16 – loader's seat.

The gun had an automatically operated wedge-type breechblock. Early-series guns had screw-type breechblocks borrowed from the 122-mm A-19 corps-level gun. The D-25T had the same recoil mechanisms as the D-5T. They were just slightly longer to reduce the heating of liquid when firing.

The gun was fired by means of an electric trigger or manually in case the electric trigger failed.

In addition to the three DT machineguns mounted like those of the IS-1, some of the IS-2s had a bracket on the cupola's rotating ring, mounting a 12.7-mm DShK machinegun developed in 1938.

The IS-2 was equipped with the 10T-17 or TSh-17 telescopic sights and PT4-17 periscopic sight. In spring 1944, the PT4-17 began to be ousted by the MK-IV vision device.

Workers inspecting a dismounted 122-mm D-25T wedge-breechblock gun in a Ukraine-based armour repairs factory, 1945.

23

IS-2

1:48

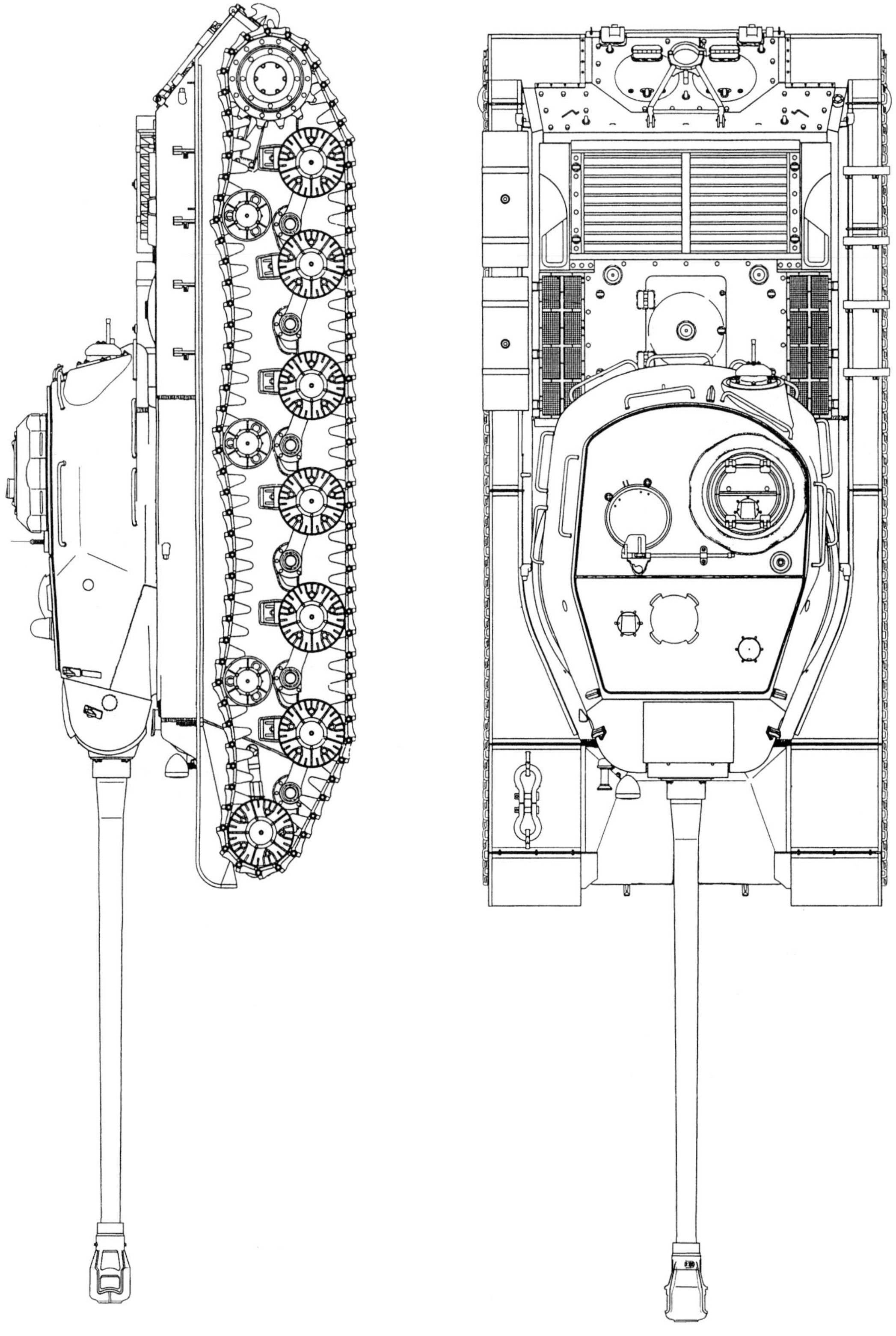

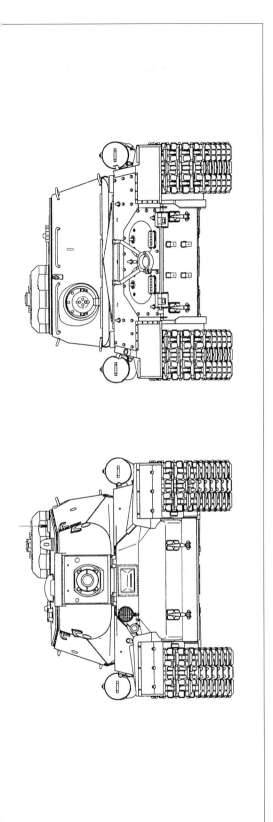

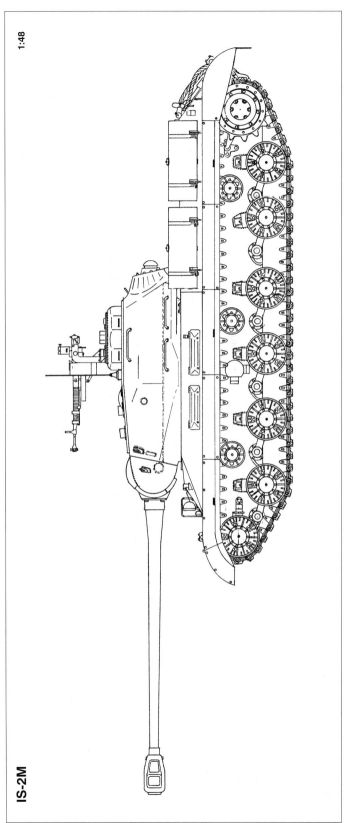

1:48

IS-2M

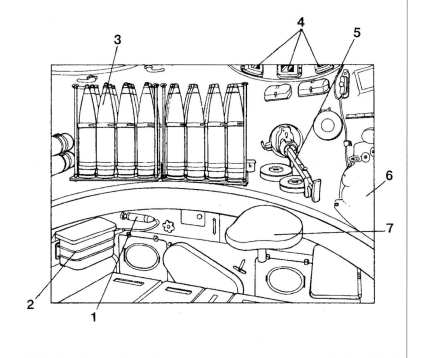

IS-2 turret rear from inside:

1 – grease-gun;
2 – kerosene/petroleum heater;
3 – ammunition stowage (projectiles);
4 – commander's vision blocks;
5 – the rear-firing DT machine gun;
6 – radio set;
7 – commander's seat.

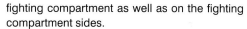

The mantlet of the 122-mm gun. The coaxial machine gun port is to the left of the gun as seen with the gunsight port on the right.

The D-25T gun's ammunition load was 28 separate loading 53-VOF-471 blast/fragmentation and 53-VBR-471 AP/tracer rounds. The DT machineguns' ammunition load comprised 2,331 rounds of ammunition, while the DShK had 250 rounds to fire. All main gun projectiles were stowed in the turret rear overhang in four stowage units, while the cases were stowed in the turret, on side racks and on the floor of the fighting compartment as well as on the fighting compartment sides.

The IS tank was powered by the 12-cylinder four-stroke V-2IS (V-2-10) diesel engine producing 520 hp at 2,000 rpm. The cylinders were set in a V-shaped layout at 60 deg. The compression ratio equalled 14-15. The engine weighed 1,000 kg.

The three fuel cells had a capacity of 520 litres. Another 300 litres of fuel were carried in three outside fuel tanks not connected to the fuel system. The engine had the pump fuel feed by means of the NK-1 fuel pump.

The tank had a pressurised circulating lubrication system, the oil tank of which was fitted with a circulation tank ensuring quick heating of oil and enabling the dilution of oil by means of petrol.

The tank was equipped with a closed-loop assisted-circulation liquid cooling system. The system included two lamellar/tubular U-shaped radiators installed above the centrifugal fan.

To purify the air fed to the engine's cylinders, the vehicle was furnished with two VT-5 'multicyclone' air filters. Their heads were fitted with injectors and sparking plugs to heat the airflow in winter.

The engine was started by the inertial starter with both manual and electric actuators or by air bottles.

Characteristics	IS-1	IS-2
All-up weight, tonnes	44	46
Crew	4	4
Dimensions, mm:		
length	8,560	9,830
width	3,070	3,070
height	2,735	2,730
ground clearance	470	470
Axis of bore, mm	1,940	1,940
Armour, mm:		
glacis plate	120-60	120
side	90	90
rear	60	60
roof	30	30
hull floor		30-20
turret		30-100
Maximum speed, km/h	37	37
Average speed, km/h:		
on road	22	22
off road	16	16
Endurance, km:		
on road	130-240	130-240
off road	110-125	110-125
Obstacles:		
gradient, degrees	36	36
ditch, m.	2.5	2.5
vertical obstacle, m	1	1
fording capability, m	1.3	1.3
Ground contact		
area, mm	4,300	4,300
Specific ground		
pressure, kg/cm^2	0.78	0.81
Specific power, hp	11.8	11.3

Ball mount of the rear-firing turret machine gun.

The electric equipment had the single-wire configuration. 24V and 12V voltage was used. The sources of power were the 1 kW generator and two batteries 128 Amps/hr each. Power was consumed by the inertial starter's 0.88 kW electric motor, turret traverse electric motor, radio, intercom, fan's electric motor, instruments, scale and sights' crosshairs illumination lamps, sound warning devices, inside and outside lighting and electric triggers of the main armament and machineguns.

All IS tanks were fitted with the 10R or 10RK simplex composite radio transceiver and TPU-4-bisF intercom for four users.

IS-2, 72nd Guards Heavy Tank Regiment, 3rd Guards Tank Army, 1st Ukrainian Front, somewhere near Lvov, July 1944.

The experimental
IS-3 (Object 244).

IS-4 (Object 245)
on summer tests,
July 1944.

However, the issue of the IS-2's armament was not settled completely after the tank had been fitted with the 122-mm main gun. The military was not very keen on it due to its low rate of fire and small ammunition load – 28 separately loading rounds. Compare this to the IS-1's 59-round and KV-1S's 114-round ammunition loads. In addition, the first encounters with hostile heavy tanks revealed that the original 122-mm BR-471 pointed armour-piercing projectile could only punch through the Panther's frontal armour at a range of 600-700 m only. The Tiger's thinner armour was penetrated from as far as 1,200 m but only well-trained gunners were able to hit the enemy at such a range. The formi-

dable OF-471 blast/fragmentation projectiles hitting German tanks could make their welding seams crack and even tear their glacis plates away from the welding seams. The early results of the IS-2's combat employment, which were proven by firing tests at the testing range in Kubinka in January 1944, compelled the designers to seek innovative solutions.

On 27 December 1943, the State Defence Committee issued a resolution on fitting the IS tank with a higher-firepower main armament. February 1944 saw the designing of three tanks, namely the IS-3, IS-4 and IS-5 (not to be mistaken for the post-World-War-2 tanks with those designations).

The IS-3 (Object 244) was the IS No.1 proto-type, whose original D-5T-85 gun was replaced with the more lethal D-5-T-85BM featuring a muzzle velocity of 900 m/s. Installation of the D-5T-85BM entailed no modifications, because the dimensions remained unchanged. Object 244 was used for testing the advanced PT-8 collapsible telescopic sight and a number of prototype engine and transmission assemblies, including 3-4 and 7-8 gear synchronisers which allowed the gear-changing time to be slashed and made the driving of the tank easier. Object 244's trials lasted until late March 1944, but failed due to the barrel's insufficient strength.

The first attempt at up-gunning the heavy tanks with a 100-mm gun was made in December 1943 by TsAKB fitting the production KV-85's upgraded turret with the S-34 main gun. The vehi-cle used to be called IS-100 in official documents. To increase the rate of fire, the fighting compartment layout had to be modified by seating the commander and the gunner to the right of the gun and the loader to the left. Hence the loader's hatch and the cupola had to swap their places. The tank was tested at the Gorokhovetsky testing ground late in January 1944. The resulting report stated: "The S-34 self-propelled/tank gun has passed its field trials comprising 638 rounds fired and 160 km covered and is fit for fielding as part of tanks and self-propelled gun systems. The trials of the S-34 proved that the KV tank's increased-ring turret dimensions allow it to house the 100-mm gun and a crew of three. " The S-34's design was debugged, and two more guns were manufactured – one to equip an IS tank and the other to fit a SU-85 SPG.

By 20 February 1944, Plant 100 had had to design and build the S-34-fitted IS tank and submit it for testing. The programme slipped behind schedule due to slippage of the gun development efforts. Therefore, the People's Commissariat for Heavy Industry decided to fit a production IS-85 with the 100-mm D-10T gun derived by Plant 9 from a self-propelled gun of the same calibre. Unlike the S-34, the derivative was fitted to the original turret without major modifications being required. From 12 March to 6 April, the IS-4 (Object 245) tank was undergoing official trials, which it failed and had to be returned to the plant

122-mm rounds' armour penetration capability*			
Range, m	500	1000	2000
BR471	150/122	138/113	118/96
BR-471B	157/128	147/120	129/105

* The first figures show the thickness of the armour penetrated at an incidence angle of 90 deg., while the second figures show that at an incidence angle of 60 deg.

IS-2 streamlined
welded nose with
attachments to
the left and right
of the towing
hooks for four
backup track
links, removed
from all ISs after
the World War 2.

The arrangement
of backup track
links on the lower
front plate of the
streamlined
welded nose of
an IS-2M.

The arrangement
of backup track
links on the lower
front plate of the
broken welded
nose of an IS-2M.

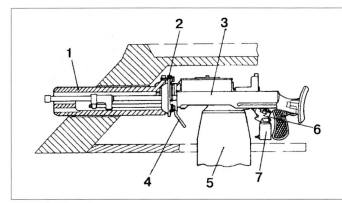

Bow machine gun:

1 – tube;
2 – hole cage;
3 – machine gun;
4 – ring clamp with handle;
5 – shell bag;
6 – trigger;
7 – machine gun trigger solenoid.

Bow machine gun. The figure probably shows a DT mockup because the barrel of a real machine gun should not protrude that far.

for debugging the gun's semi-automatic gear and several other components. As a result, the tank had to be fitted with the D-10T gun semi-automatic gear, a more powerful fighting compartment ventilator, a modified ammo stowage area in the turret's rear overhang, etc. The gun had a muzzle velocity of 900 m/s. The ammunition load was made up of 30 fixed rounds with 15.6-kg armour-piercing and blast/fragmentation projectiles.

Plant 92 supplied the S-34 gun to Plant 100 in early April 1944 instead of 20 February as was planned. The manufacture of the new turret was slow too. Unlike its rival, the IS-5 featured an upside-down mantlet since the gunner was seated on the right. The cupola and commander's seat were shifted to the right side of the turret too. The loader was seated to the left of the gun. In addition to the crew of three, the mechanical ram-

mer and the sight's stabiliser were to be installed in the turret. The improvements resulted in Plant 100 completing the IS-5 (Object 248) as late as June 1944.

From 1 to 6 July, the joint testing of the IS-4 and IS-5 tanks was underway at the Gorokhovetsky testing ground, during which the military rejected the former and suggested the latter be modified. By October, the rammer and vertically stabilised sight had been installed in the IS-5's turret. The ammunition load had grown to 39 rounds. The commander's station had been moved closer to the right side of the turret to prevent the breech from hitting the commander when recoiling. The trials proved that the tank's combat capabilities had grown considerably. It was second to none among the then known tanks in terms of rate of fire. The same went for its armour penetration and fire accuracy on the move. However, the top

brass decided against launching the IS-5's full-rate production. Instead, the designers were asked to develop a new round with higher armour penetration capability to be fired by the 122-mm D-25T. Such a round – the blunt-nosed armour-piercing BR-471B – was developed in spring 1945 but only started entering heavy tanks' ammunition loads after the war had finished.

However, the issue of stepping up the armour penetration capability became irrelevant in autumn 1944. The D-25T suddenly became extremely effective against German tanks. Line units sometimes reported cases when 122-mm BR-471 projectiles fired from over 2,500 m away would ricochet off Panthers' glacis armour, leaving huge fractures in it. This was because in summer 1944 the Germans lacked manganese by and had to use high-carbon nickel-doped steel that was very fragile, especially where the welding seams ran.

Right:
IS-2s of the 71st
Guards Heavy
Tank Regiment on
the Sandomir
Bridgehead,
August 1944.

Opposite: IS-2s
of the 27th
Separate Guards
Heavy Tank
Regiment
entering Vyborg,
June 1944.

IS-2, 64th Guards Heavy Tank Regiment, 3rd Guards Mechanised Corps, 1st Baltic Front, somewhere near Siauliai, July 1944.

The first encounters with enemy tanks highlighted the insufficient armour protection provided by the IS tanks' glacis plate. Early in 1944, attempts were made to strengthen the hull's armour protection by tempering the armour to make it extremely hard. However, this resulted in a sharp rise in the hull components' rigidity. When an IS tank made in March 1944 was shot at by a 76-mm ZIS-3 gun from 500-600 m away at a testing ground, its armour cracked on all sides, with the bulk of rounds failing to penetrate it but generating, however, much spall. This explains the heavy losses of IS-85s and IS-122s in winter and spring 1944.

In February 1944, Central Research Institute 48 (TsNII-48) was tasked with researching the IS tank's hull armour strength. The research proved that, with the existing shape of the glacis plate, it would survive hits by German 75-mm and 88-mm projectiles only if it was at least 145-150 mm thick, i. e. 20-30 mm more than the existing thickness. On TsNII-48's advice, the tempering regimes were altered and the glacis plate was modified.

IS-2 advancing to Riga, September 1944.

The new hull, featuring the so-called "straightened nose", retained the earlier armour thickness. The driver's hatch that had degraded the glacis plate's strength was removed. The new glacis plate itself was slanted at 60 deg. relative to the vertical, which made it resistant to the projectiles of German 88-mm KwK 36 main guns even at point-blank range and at ±30-deg. incidence. The lower glacis plate with armour at 30 degrees remained vulnerable. To increase its protection, the driving compartment had to be redesigned considerably. However, since the lower glacis plate's hit probability was lower than that for the rest of the hull, the designers decided to let it be. To strengthen the lower glacis plate, spare track links were mounted on it between the towing hooks on 15 July 1944. Uralmashzavod switched over to the welded straightened-nose hulls in May 1944 while Plant 200 launched production of cast straightened-nose hulls in June 1944. The tanks with both old and new hulls continued to be made concurrently until the backlog of hulls was used up.

IS-2 in the Baltic.
1st Baltic Front,
July 1944.

Loader's hatch
cover:
1 – torsion bar;
2 – hatch hinge;
3 – bracket;
4 – hatch hold-
open lock;
5 – lock handle;
6 – lock stopper.

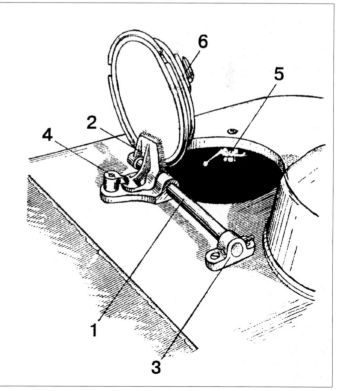

As far as the turret was concerned, stepping up its armour protection proved to be impossible. Designed to accommodate the 85-mm gun, it was statically balanced. After the 122-mm gun was installed, the imbalance moment reached 1,000 km/m. In addition, the performance specifications called for the frontal armour protection to increase to 130 mm, which would have tipped the balance even more, necessitating a new traverse mechanism. Since doing all that without a radical redesigning of the turret was impossible, the idea was discarded.

The IS tank's configuration changed considerably during production. There were roughly six versions of the tank based on the design and production modifications introduced.

The first variant was the baseline production IS-1 armed with the 85-mm main gun and three DT machineguns. For the sake of the hull's enhanced armour survivability and ease of production, some of these vehicles had the midsection of their 'broken' bows slanted at a higher angle (75 deg. compared to the previous 72 deg.) as well as the length of the casting's sides reduced and the track adjuster's attachment to the hull side.

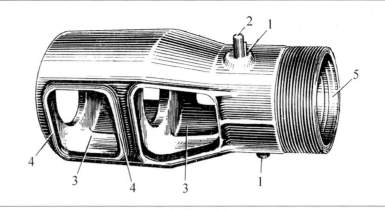

Wedge-
breechblock D-25
muzzle brake:

1 – eye;
2 – stopper;
3 – windows;
4 – diaphragm;
5 – screw.

In the assembly
workshop,
Kirovsky Zavod,
Chelyabinsk,
December 1944.

The second version had the same running gear as the IS-1, but a new turret had to be developed owing to stet tank's D-25 screw-type breechblock gun with the German-type twin-chamber muzzle brake. It differed from the IS-1's turret in having the cupola and the periscopic sight's armoured cover shifted to the left, bulged turret side on the left, gun's elongated armour protection cone and a hub on the mantlet.

The third variant was identical to the first one, except D-25 wedge-type breechblock main gun with an advanced muzzle brake.

The fourth version resulted from the permission granted to Plant 200 to carry on using old hulls from its backlog during transition to 'straightened bow' production. Some of this variant's hulls had six track links attached to the lower glacis plate. To fit the TSh-17 sight, the mantlet had to be redesigned. Its left side was extended and the left side of the armoured protection cone was stretched forward. The PT4-17 sight was replaced with the MK-IV observation device. The early-series vehicles had two ports to fit the 10T-17 and TSh-17 sights. In addition, the early turrets had handrails welded low down but they were discarded later.

The fifth and sixth versions featured heavily redesigned 'straight nose' hulls. The fifth variant's hull from Plant 200 featured the straightened cast bow and old fighting compartment casting. The sixth version made by UZTM had the straightened bow welded to the hull and a new turret fighting compartment casting. Almost all hulls of the fifth and sixth IS variants had six spare track links attached to the lower glacis plate. The rear upper plate featured a hinged bracket to hold the gun in the travelling position, with the left side of the hull being fitted with an ammunition resupply hatch. Those tanks were equipped with a full set of then-advanced cast track support rollers with three lightening holes.

In addition to upgrading the tank during full-scale production, the Kirovsky plant and Plant 100 were designing advanced vehicles in line with specification requirements devised by the Main Armoured Directorate in late 1943. Mention should be made of the draft design of the IS-2M heavy tank, proposed by a design team led by N. F. Shamshurin in spring 1944. The tank featured a very unorthodox configuration, with its fighting compartment, turret and transmission situated in the rear of the hull, the engine compartment in the middle and the driving compartment at the front. The running gear comprised large-diameter roadwheels without support rollers. Torque was transferred from the engine to the transmission by the driveshaft running under the floor of the fighting compartment. Placing the turret on the rear of the hull prevented the long-barrelled main armament from sticking into the ground and made it easier for the tank to manoeu-

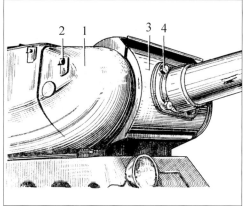

D-25 gun (IS-2) armour protection:

1 – turret front casing;
2 – lifting hook;
3 – gun mantlet;
4 – bolts securing mantlet to internal gun cradle.

vre in narrow passageways. Then, early in summer 1944, Plant 100's design outfit began designing of two versions of the IS-6 heavy tank (in-house designations Object 252 and Object 253), while the IS-2M programme was terminated.

In addition, the large-diameter stamped road-wheels designed to fit Object 252 were tested on the Object 244 prototype loaded with pig iron to ensure the weight required.

On 5 August 1944, Plant 100 was awarded an Order of Lenin for its contribution to developing advanced IS heavy tanks and self-propelled guns. The Kirovsky plant in Chelyabinsk got an Order of the Red Star for its role in introducing into production advanced tanks, SPGs and tank diesel engines as well as fielding them with the Red Army. February 1946 saw Zh. Ya. Kotin, A. S. Yermolayev, G. N. Moskvin, N. F. Shamshurin, G. N. Rybin, A. S. Schneideman, Ye. P. Dedov and K. N. Ilyin awarded the Stalin Prize.

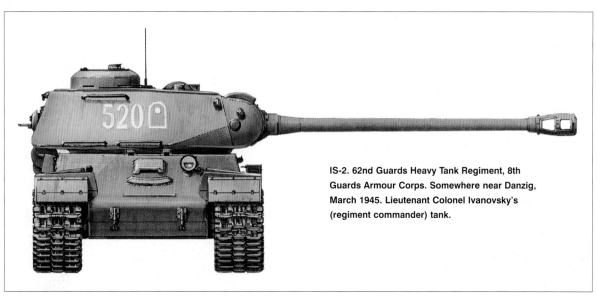

IS-2. 62nd Guards Heavy Tank Regiment, 8th Guards Armour Corps. Somewhere near Danzig, March 1945. Lieutenant Colonel Ivanovsky's (regiment commander) tank.

IS-2 in Mlawa,
Poland, winter
1945.

IS TANKS IN COMBAT

In February 1944, the Red Army's shock regiments operating KV tanks were given a new TO&E (Table of organisation and equipment). At the same time, the Red Army started activating new units termed heavy tank regiments and fielded with IS tanks. While still at the activation stage, the new regiments were designated as Guards. Under the TO&E, each new regiment's strength was 375 personnel, four IS tank companies operating a total of 24 vehicles, a submachinegunner company, a maintenance support company, an antiaircraft battery, an engineer's platoon, a logistics platoon and the regimental medical aid station. The activation took place in the Tesnitsky tank camp near Tula. The IS heavy tank's crew featured two commissioned officers (commander and senior driver) and two sergeants (gunner and loader/junior driver). Such crewing highlighted the importance of the missions handled by the new tanks and the Guards regiments operating them. Unfortunately, only a small number of crewmen had fought in the KV and Churchill heavy tanks and gained a relevant combat experience. Mostly, the personnel would come right out of military schools, with some of them having a bit of extra training at the Kirovsky plant. The Main Armoured Directorate would attach its officers to the regiments deploying to the front to observe the operation of new tanks.

The first three regiments – 1st, 29th and 58th – reported to the commander of the 1st Guards Army that served the main attack in the Proskurov-Chernovtsy offensive operation. Another two regiments – 8th and 13th – were assigned to the 2nd Guards Tank Army and were among the units that bore the brunt of the main attack of the Wehrmacht's 16th, 17th and 1st Panzer Divisions trying to raise the blockade of the German force encircled by the Red Army near the city of Korsun-Shevchenkovsky.

The 13th Guards Heavy Tank Shock Regiment was among the first units to go into action. With its 21 IS-85 tanks, it arrived in the vicinity of Fastov and Belaya Tserkov on 15 February 1944. Having completed its approach, the regiment was tasked with supporting the attack of the 109th Tank Brigade on the village of Lisyanka. The regimental OC allocated a five-tank company to this end. By the time it was committed, 109th Tank's last T-34s attacking the village head-on had been damaged by German Panthers and antitank and assault guns. Having let the IS tanks come up as close as 600-800 m, the German tanks and SPGs opened up, damaging all of the attacking heavy tanks within 10 minutes, with two of them burning out completely. Each IS-85 took three to seven hits. Lisyanka was encircled and taken on the next day. The troops seized 16 Panthers, two Pz. IVs and two assault guns abandoned by the Germans due to a lack of fuel.

On 5 March 1944, 15 IS-85s of the 13th Guards Heavy Tank Shock Regiment were supporting the 50th Tank Brigade's attack on Uman. Five tanks were lost to the enemy's 88-mm flak guns, three malfunctioned and one rolled off a bridge and overturned near the village of Polkovnichye. An unusual event happened there as well: an IS-85 had its lower glacis plate punched through by a projectile fired by a German s.Pz.B. 41 heavy anti-tank rifle with a 28/20-mm conical barrel.

The IS-85's first recorded encounter with Tigers took place on 4 March 1944 near the town of Starokonstantinovo in Ukraine during the Proskurov-Chernovtsy offensive operation. The 1st Guards Heavy Tank Shock Regiment led by Col. N. I. Bulanov clashed with a Tiger tank company of the sPzAbt (Heavy Tank Battalion) 503. The skirmish in low visibility conditions at a range of 1,500-1,800 resulted in an IS-85 destroyed and three damaged (they were repaired later). The return fire damaged the main gun of one Tiger and the running gear of another. On 16 March, Tigers ambushed four IS tanks, two of which

burnt out together with their crews. A bit earlier, on 8 March, two IS tanks were shot up in an ambush sprung by camouflaged 75-mm assault guns from a range of 150-200 m. One of the tanks was hit eight times and the other four times.

These battles resulted in the Main Armoured Directorate concluding that the IS-85's weapons and armour protection were no match for those of the German tanks. The report advised the glacis plate shape and armour protection be modified and armament be beefed up. The documents of the time prove that, of the total number of the heavy tanks of the type, exactly one hundred saw action. Another six were sent to higher armour officer schools – two vehicles each. One tank (No.31113) was used for testing at the testing ground in Kubinka. By the end of the war, 37 IS-85s were still in service in good running order. Another 37 were written off in April 1945 due to natural wear and tear, because each logged a mileage exceeding 2,000 km.

The IS-2 proved to be a more formidable opponent to the Wehrmacht's tanks, because its D-25T main armament featured a greater flat-trajectory range than the D-5T, while its armour-piercing ammunition boasted a far greater armour penetration capability. Its powerful 122-mm blast/fragmentation ammunition was effective against German tanks too.

Poznan greets Soviet tank units. February 1945.

In Stargard, Pomerania, 2nd Belorussian Front, 19 March 1945, lacking a turret-mounted machine gun, the crew used a DT on an infantry bipod to counter German soldiers with Panzerschrecke.

Encounters between IS-2s and Tigers were rare. Not more than 10 such encounters, including encounters with Tiger IIs, have been recorded in the battles fought by German heavy tank battalions. Of these operations of the 71st Independent Guards Heavy-Tank Regiment in the first-series IS-122 tanks are of special interest. In conjunction with the 6th Guards Tank Corps, the regiment participated in defeating a King Tiger battalion in the vicinity of Sandomir in August 1944. This is how it was described by the Regimental Combat Operations Report for 14 July - 31 August 1944:

"In the morning of 13 August 1944, the regiment launched an attack towards Oglenduv in conjunction with the 289th Rifle Regiment, 97th Rifle Division. The fire of hostile tanks at the outskirts of Oglenduv stopped the advancing infantry in its tracks. Then, the tank platoon led by Guards Senior Lieutenant Klimenkov advanced to the prepared positions and opened up on the enemy tanks. In a brief encounter, Guards Sr. Lt. Klimenkov destroyed one enemy tank and damaged another, these being the first enemy King Tiger tanks destroyed. This done, the infantry burst into Oglenduv encountering no stiff opposition. At the same time, seven King Tiger tanks attacked our positions from Hill 272.1. The tank of

Guards Sr. Lt. Udalov, lying in ambush in the bushes east of Mokre, allowed them as close as 700-800 m and opened up on the leading one. It took Udalov several accurate shots to set it afire and damage another one. When the enemy tanks carried on and started to move off, Udalov took a shorter road via the woods to meet them there and opened fire on them at the edge of the woods. Having lost another burning hulk, the enemy retreated. However, the King Tigers repeated their attack soon, attacking towards Ponik where the tank of Guards Lt. Belyakov sat in ambush. Belyakov engaged the enemy from a range of 1,000. The third round fired set a King Tiger ablaze, with the rest turning their tails. Thus, the tankers, assisted by artillerists, repulsed seven enemy attacks, having inflicted heavy personnel and materiel losses.

"The experience has proven that the IS-122 tank has a marching capability of 70-100 km/day at an average road speed of 20-25 km/h and a dirt track speed of 10-15 km/h. The endurance is 125-150 km. On average, the tanks have covered 1,100 km, having produced 270 engine-hours instead of the guaranteed 150 engine-hours. The operational speed in rugged terrain equals 8-12 km/h. The main armament's practicable rate of fire is 2-3 rd/min. One ammunition load is enough

Soviet soldiers near an IS-2 damaged in action in Pomerania, March 1945.

Tanks of the 29th
Guards Heavy
Tank Regiment at
the line of
departure, 1st
Ukrainian Front,
1945

87th Guards
Heavy Tank
Regiment, 1st
Ukrainian Front,
Breslau, April
1945 with the
tank crew
(commander
B. I. Degtyarev)
relaxing after a
battle.

for one day of offensive operations. Firing and observation conditions in the tank are mostly satisfactory. It has turned out that the periscopic sight is inconvenient for firing and observation because it lacks a 360-deg. capability and is unusable for firing because it is difficult to adjust and its crosshairs are difficult to move quickly. The existing cast armour is penetrated by 88-mm ammunition from a range of 800-1,000 m due to its low quality, e. g. low density and bubbles.

"Conclusion:

"The IS-122 tank's armament is the most formidable among all existing tanks. The 122-mm projectile features a high armour penetration capability, which makes the tank the best means of combating the enemy's tank.

"Its deficiency is the heavy smoke generated by firing which reveals the tank's position.

"The defensive operations on the River Vistula bridgehead proved that enemy tanks always steered clear of the IS-122s' defensive positions and, as a result, often had to alter the direction of their attacks, probing for vulnerable frontages defended by lighter tanks."

The 26th and 27th Independent Guards Heavy Tank Regiments were manned and deployed to the Leningrad Front in early May

1944, where they fought in the Vyborg (vs Finland) operation, and the 31st Regiment took part in the Narva (vs Germany) operation. The enemy had well-fortified defences there, with its forested swampy terrain being inaccessible in summer. Nonetheless, by late 10 June (the first day of the offensive), the 27th Regiment had made 14 km along the Vyborg Motorway, then penetrated the second and third defensive areas and took the city and fortress of Vyborg on 20 June. This feat earned it the honorary title 'Vyborgsky' (Russian for 'of Vyborg'). During the following 11 days, the regiment covered another 110 km at an average speed of 10 km a day. Then, the 26th, 27th, 31st and 76th Independent Guards Heavy Tank Regiments were redeployed to the area adjacent to the east of the Baltic where the 3rd, 15th, 32nd, 35th, 64th, 75th and 81st Regiments were fighting. A peculiarity of the hostilities in the area was the enemy's lack of a continuous forward edge of the battle area (FEBA), with terrain characterised by numerous swamps, woods and rivers posing a serious problem. On the final leg of the march towards the assembly area, the 64th Regiment tankers had to pull two IS-2s one after the other out of small rivers into which they had sunk during crossings.

The Germans laid numerous minefields on armour approaches. Nine of the 35th Regiment IS tanks hit landmines in 10 days in October alone. Eight of them were later repaired by the regimental workshop. The 31st Regiment lost 13 vehicles to landmines and another six to Panzerpatrone rocket launchers from 17 to 26 September during the battle of Tallinn. During the 16 October offensive of Memel, the 75th Regiment lost three IS-2s to a minefield during the very first attack.

During the Tallinn operation, the 26th Independent Guards Heavy Tank Regiment fought to cover over 620 km and destroyed three enemy tanks, seven artillery batteries and eight mortar batteries from 17 to 24 September while losing five commissioned officers and seven sergeants KIA, three tanks destroyed and 10 damaged, of which four were in need of overhaul.

The situation in East Prussia was even more complicated. East Prussia's defences had been developed for a long time, with the fortifications included specially equipped village houses making up integrated defensive areas. In such a situation, the 81st Regiment was fighting near Klein Degesen on 16 October 1944, with six of its IS-2s getting hit 12-19 times (six hits punched through the armour). Tigers had been springing ambushes

Off with the Panzerschrecke! The 62nd Guards Heavy Tank Regiment in urban warfare in Danzig, March 28, 1945.

from a range of 800-1,200 m and firing until Soviet tanks caught fire. The bitterest battle took place on 20 October when the regiment advancing towards the town of Stallupönen faced stiff resistance put up by dug-in hostile tanks and antitank guns. The Soviet tankers destroyed three Tigers and 10 guns in that battle, while suffering heavy losses themselves – seven IS-2s were burnt out and one damaged by enemy gunners.

Having repaired its damaged material and been re-supplied, the 81st Regiment carried on with its advance via East Prussia. As of 14 February, it operated 21 tanks in good running order, with one being in need of overhaul and one being a write-off.

On 15 February 1945, the 81st Regiment as part of the 144th Rifle Division attacked the enemy near Nemritten and seized its southern part in a 30-min. battle. Towards evening, the town was seized by a joint armour and infantry attack. During the battle, the tankers had destroyed two enemy tanks, four guns and an artillery battery with its crews, having lost one IS-2 burnt and three damaged.

On the next night, 16 of the regiment's tanks launched an attack on Kukehnen. The 144 Rifle Division's commander did not order the enemy weapons to be suppressed, believing the heavy tanks were able to take care of themselves. Having faced heavy flanking fire, the regiment lost four IS-2 tanks (two burnt out and two damaged). Three reached the western outskirts of the town and stopped there, since the infantry lagged behind. While there, another two vehicles were damaged. The tankers fought enemy infantry, tanks and artillery pieces for more than three hours, having repeatedly retreated to gee the sluggish infantry and make it follow them. Having lost nine tanks as damaged, the regiment was ordered back by the 72nd Rifle Corps's commander at dusk. On 17 February, the regiment was fixing and servicing its tanks. The unit retained 15 vehicles, of which seven were operational, two needed mid-life repair, three were to be recovered and three had to be written off. Towards evening, the operational control of the regiment was given to the officer commanding (OC) the 120th Tank Brigade. In conjunction with the 120th Tank Brigade, the 81st Regiment attacked Albenlauk on 19 February and took it after a 40-min. battle. Exploiting the success, the regiment fought towards the railway station of Kukehnen on 21 and 22 February and evenrually seized it.

Fighting in East Prussia, the regiment accomplished 83 tank attacks from 15 to 27 February 1945, losing five commissioned officers and 11 other ranks KIA, 17 officers and eight other ranks WIA and five IS-2s burnt and 16 damaged (mostly by the fire of Tigers and 88-mm antitank guns).

IS-2. 1st
Belorussian
Front, Berlin,
April 1945.

Soviet tankers destroyed four enemy tanks, four armoured personnel carriers, 19 machinegun crews and an ammunition dump and captured an assault gun. As of 2 March 1945, there were two tanks left in the regiment, of which only one was operational.

Tankers with the 80th Independent Guards Heavy-Tank Regiment fought in the Vistula-Oder operation more successfully. None of its 23 IS-2s suffered irreparable battle damage between 14 and 31 January 1945, while the regiment destroyed 19 enemy tanks and self-propelled guns, 41 guns, 15 machinegun nests, 10 mortars and 12 dugouts.

The 33rd Independent Guards Heavy Tank Regiment lost only three tanks in the Vistula-Oder operation, though on the very first day of the offensive, 14 January, it broke through both the first and second lines of defence of the German 9th Army and made 22km headway. Exploiting the success, the regiment fought its way for four more days, covering another 120 km. Having penetrated the Meseritz fortified area, the unit entered Germany in conjunction with the 69th Army on 29 January and reached the River Oder near Frankfurt an der Oder on 3 February, covering 70 km a further.

It is worth mentioning that the Germans had for a long time been unable to get a close look at damaged IS-2s because the battlefields were owned by the Soviets. They got such an opportunity only in May 1944 near the Romanian town of Targul Frumos.

Activation of independent Guards heavy tank brigades kicked off in December 1944. Normally, they would be the former T-34 brigades. Activation was prompted by the need to concentrate the heavy tanks on the cutting edge of main attacks conducted by the fronts and armies to penetrate the enemy's well-fortified defences and fight its tank formations. An independent heavy-tank brigade's TO&E included three heavy-tank regiments, a motorised sub-machinegunner battalion and support and maintenance elements – in all, 1,666 personnel, 65 IS-2 tanks, three SU-76 SPGs, 19 APCs and three armoured cars. A total of five such brigades were formed.

As the war came to a close, each armoured corps had at least one IS-2 regiment attached, with the IS-2s' role in assaulting well-fortified urban areas in Germany and East Prussia being hard to overestimate. The 122-mm main armament of the IS-2 was the ideal weapon to knock

Left above: IS-2 of the 7th Guards Heavy Tank Brigade in Berlin, May 1945.

IS-2 on the offensive, 1st Belorussian Front, Brandenburg, 1945.

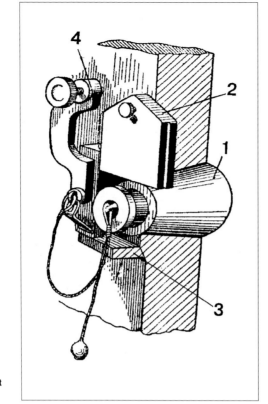

Small arms porthole lock:

1 – plug;
2 – armour plate;
3 – board;
4 – latch.

IS-2s of the 4th Heavy Tank Regiment of the Polish Army, West Pomerania, 1945.

out enemy pillboxes. A single high-explosive (HE) projectile was enough for the IS-2 to crack a machinegun nest's armoured cover, which the 85-mm gun was unable to do, and to break old buildings' heavy-duty brick masonry into smithereens. The main enemy of Soviet tanks proved to be a hostile infantryman toting a Faustpatrone, Panzerfaust or Panzerschreck rocket launcher. Red Army soldiers who were not too well versed in German designations would call all types of the weapon 'Faustpatrone' ('faust' in short) and the Wehrmacht soldiers operating them 'Faustnik'. Rocket launchers claimed up to 70% of the tanks damaged in urban-area battles. In early 1945, Soviet troops started fitting their combat vehicles with skirts to protect them from shaped charges. The skirts were made by repair personnel from thin metal sheets, meshes and even concertina wire flattened by tanks' tracks. A Faustpatrone shaped charge would tear a skirt into pieces but leave only a small melted crater on the armour. Tankers, who were partial to the gallows humour of people looking death in the face all the time, dubbed such craters 'witch's lovebites'.

Unfortunately, skirts would often be torn off or deformed by explosions and pieces of masonry. The consequences were described by Guards

IS-2 in an infantry fire support operation. The unit commander, Hero of the Soviet Union, Guards Captain Lopatkin, Berlin, 27 April, 1945.

Lt. Col. V. Mindlin, the officer commanding the 11th Independent Guards Heavy Tank Regiment during the assault on Berlin, in his book *The Last Battle is the Hardest One*:

"Here is a tank with its hatches battened down. One can hear the whining of the dynamo-tor of its radio but the crew responds neither to banging on the armour, nor to radio calls. There is a small, penny-sized melt hole in the turret. It is even too small for a small finger to get into it. A Faust's job. The skirt here was torn off and the shaped charge hit the armour.

IS-2 7th Guards Heavy Tank Brigade, Berlin, May 1945.

"The welding torch is spitting bluish fire. Only the torch can open a hatch locked from inside.

"The bodies of the four dead crewmen are being taken out of the turret. Young lads. Might have lived on.

"The shaped charge burnt through the steel armour, bursting into the tank as a fiery whirlwind. Molten steel droplets killed everyone. Neither the stowage, nor fuel cells, nor mechanisms were damaged, the people alone died. Here they are lying by the tracks of their combat vehicle lined up for the last time.

"And the tank is all right. It is sitting in the middle of the street, having lowered its main gun to the ground as if grieving about its dead crew.

"And the crew has gone.

"He who saw an armoured battle knows how horribly tankers die.

"If a projectile or a Faustpatrone hits the stowage compartment or fuel cells, the tank fireballs instantly, leaving nothing alive inside and around itself and sparing the crew horrible pain.

"However, sometimes a projectile or a Faustpatrone punches through the armour, the crew are wounded, the vehicle is on fire, the fire is nearing the stowage and fuel cells, with the crew being unable to put it out. The crew has to abandon their tank and rush as far away as possible from it before it explodes, but opening the hatches is beyond the wounded tankers' power.

"And you can hear the cries of the people burning alive. You cannot help them because the hatches are locked from inside and you can only open them with a welding torch.

"There is no battle cruoler than armoured battle. There is no more horrible death than that in a burning tank."

Fighting in an urban area with hatches open was prohibited because a hand grenade could be thrown out of any window. Therefore, the crews were ordered to close the hatches without battening them down. This allowed the number of KIAs to drop somewhat.

A special technique dubbed 'little fir-tree' was used to fight on the streets. Tanks operated in pairs and supported one another with fire. A tank platoon of two IS-2s would cover a whole street, one taking care of the right side of the street and the other of the left side. The pair of tanks would roll down the street in echelon formation, a vehicle on each side of the street. Another pair would follow and support it with fire.

Every tank company was reinforced with a submachinegun-armed infantry platoon of five squads, each assigned a tank to protect. The infantrymen would ride on the tanks, dismount when meeting the enemy and fight in conjunction with the tank they were assigned to protect. It is they who bore the brunt of taking out 'Faustniks'.

The DShK heavy machinoguns proved to be effective enough against enemy rocket-launcher gunners. However, their upwards-tilted barrels would snag various wires, especially tram power lines, tear them off and drag them along. Therefore, some DShKs were dismounted from tanks.

During the Battle of Berlin, IS tanks and SPGs served as a kind of battering ram, their formidable main guns smashing the buildings turned into fortifications. The intensity of the street fighting was so great that tank crews would use two to three ammunition loads a day. Losses suffered on the outskirts of Berlin and in the city were heavy.

Our cause is just, and here we are! Tank regiment personnel hearing Iosef Stalin's Victory Order, Berlin, May 1945. In the foreground is a welded-front IS-2, its hull made by Uralmashzavod.

Assigning combat
missions to the
officers of the 4th
Polish Heavy
Tank Regiment,
Germany, April
1945.

The 72nd Guards
Heavy Tank
Regiment in
Prague, 9 May,
1945.

For example, the 7th Guards Heavy Tank Brigade lost 131 personnel KIA and 266 WIA, 28 IS-2s burnt out by enemy antitank guns and tanks and 11 by Faustpatrone gunners, and 28 tanks damaged (later, they were repaired) during the Battle of Berlin from 16 April to 2 May 1945 alone.

During the same period, the brigade destroyed 35 enemy tanks and SPGs, 27 field guns, 17 pillboxes, left over 800 personnel casualties, captured three enemy tanks, 10 flak guns, 82 planes, 200 POWs and 57 steam engines, liberated three concentration camps and seized more than 46 villages and five cities and towns.

During the Battle of Berlin, the 67th Guards Heavy Tank Brigade lost 122 personnel KIA and 221 WIA. Twelve of its IS-2s were burnt out by enemy artillery and tanks and another 18 by 'Faustniks'. Forty-one damaged tanks were later repaired. The brigade destroyed 28 hostile tanks and SPGs, 84 field guns, 19 artillery batteries, 16 antiaircraft batteries, 52 lorries, 246 machinegun crews, 950 mortars and left upwards of 3,500 personnel casualties. Five tanks, 900 aircraft and 8,000 POWs were captured.

Bitter fighting continued until the last hours of the war. On the morning of 27 April, an IS-2 with an assault team of the 34th Independent Guards Heavy Tank Regiment hit a landmine in front of a church on Kurfürstenstrasse. It was left behind there along with the eight-man infantry squad it carried. They were opposed by about a hundred SS troops. The loader and the gunner were killed, then the tank commander was killed by a Faustpatrone, and the driver, Sgt. Herman Shashkov, kept on fighting alone. Another Faustpatrone set the engine compartment on fire. Backing out, Shashkov hit a wall that crumbled and thus put out the fire. Locked up inside the tank, the sergeant had kept on firing the main gun and machineguns until he ran out of ammunition. Then he resorted to hand grenades. When Soviets re-captured the tank, they found the partly burnt and wounded Shashkov lying on the floor of his tank with a knife in his hand.

On 30 April, the fighting was going on right by the Reichstag. In the morning, the 88th Heavy Tank Regiment crossed the River Spree via the surviving Moltke Bridge and assumed firing positions on the Kronprinzenufer Embankment. At 1300 hours, the tanks opened direct fire at the Reichstag as part of the general softening up preceding the assault. At 1830 hours, the regiment provided fire support to the second assault on the Reichstag, ceasing fire only after the fighting moved into the building itself.

In addition to the Red Army, the IS-2 was in service with the Polish Army. Seventy-one tanks were transferred to the 4th and 5th Heavy Tank Regiments when they were being activated. During the fighting in Pomerania, the 4th Regiment destroyed 31 enemy tanks while losing 14 of its own. Both regiments fought in the Battle of Berlin.

An IS-2 column
on the move,
Turkestan Military
District, 1950.

Opposite:
IS-2s of a
composite tank
regiment in Gorky
Street, Moscow,
during the Victory
Parade, 24 June,
1945.

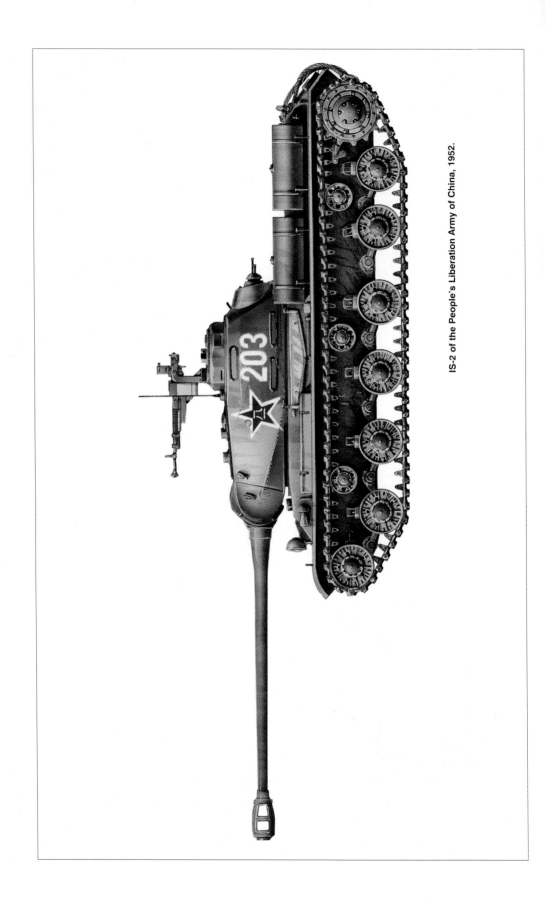

IS-2 of the People's Liberation Army of China, 1952.

Two more such regiments – the 6th and 7th – were to be formed, but the war ended before that was done. By the end of the war, the Polish Army had had 26 IS-2s (21 vehicles had been returned to the Red Army) that made up the Polish 7th Heavy Tank Regiment after the war.

The Czechoslovak Army took delivery of several IS-2s in spring 1945 on the eve of the liberation of Prague.

The IS-2 production was discontinued the same year. Finally, 10 tanks were made by the Leningrad-located Kirovsky plant in its rebuilt workshops.

Minsk, 1 May, 1952, during a military parade. In the foreground is an early IS-2. The tank to the right has a German-design muzzle brake and the MK-IV sight instead of the PT4-17 periscope.

IS-2 of the 7th Heavy Tank Regiment of the Polish Army during a military parade in Lublin, July 1954.

An IS-2M in a
Minsk World
War 2 museum. It
is an early
version of the hull
with a driver's
plug hatch.

In the early 1950s, a small number of IS-2s were handed over to China. By the end of the Korean War, Chinese volunteers had operated 38 IS-2s; however, little is known of their combat record.

Cuba got two IS-2 regiments in the early 1960s. According to the foreign press, the tanks have been in service with the coastal defence force.

About the same time, IS-2s were supplied to the Democratic People's Republic of Korea (DPRK). North Korea operated two armoured divisions, each including a heavy-tank regiment.

The IS-2 remained in the Red Army's inventory after World War 2. The IS-3 (Object 703) intended to replace it had grave deficiencies hampering its field operation. The number of IS-3s built was small. Its production was terminated in 1956. The IS-4 (Object 701) proved to be difficult to operate and maintain, too. At the same time, the Army was quite content with the IS-2 – a reliable and easy-to-operate combat vehicle. Therefore, the Main Armoured Directorate decided that IS-2s would be improved during overhaul starting in 1957 to extend their service life, as well as commonising a number of their units and assemblies with those of other heavy tanks.*

Later, the IS-2 was re-engined with the V-54K-IS motor with the electric starter, NIKS-1 injector-type preheater, MZN-2 electric oil pump and VTI-2 air filtering mechanism.

The re-engining caused modification of the lubricating and cooling systems. The external fuel tanks were incorporated into the fuel system in a manner similar to that of the IS-3. The IS-2 was fitted with a gearbox, with an oil pump, and an oil cooling system, and a rigid fastening to the rear support was introduced.

The planetary steering gears were connected to the clutches of the final drives by means of semi-rigid joints. The running gear was furnished with advanced roadwheels and nonadjustable-bearing drive sprockets.

As far as the hull was concerned, the main changes were to engine compartment, including the introduction of a reinforced motor base and advanced gearbox supports. In addition, the driver's slit-type vision device was replaced by the prismatic observation device from the T-54 tank, and the IS-2 was equipped with the Ugol device and TVN-2 or BVN night vision device.

---

* Limited IS-2 modernisation efforts started in 1954, e. g. strengtnening the bottom of the hull under the gearbox by welding a 16-20-mm armour plate to it.

An IS-2M in the Moscow Poklonnaya Gora World War 2 museum. The TVN-2 night sight cell is above the observation slit in the front armour plate. Large brackets in the rear accommodate two 200-litre fuel drums, with smaller brackets in-between – for smoke dischargers. The travelling-position gun bracket is on the centre of the rear plate. The rear-facing turret machine gun is dismounted and its ball bearing welded up.

A new reinforced turret lock similar to that of the T-54 and a gun elevation mechanism with a jammed-gun release device were installed in the turret. The main gun's ammunition load increased to 35 rounds. The machinegun in the rear of the turret was replaced with an additional fan. A special armour patch was welded over the machinegun's port. The patch featured a labyrinth slit for ventilation.

The number of batteries doubled from two to four. The tank also got post-war-designed R-113 radios and R-120 intercom; new wings with bunkers similar to those of the IS-3, dual-hatted as skirts; electric fuses and electric ejectors for BDSh smoke canisters and a second searchlight with a blackout device. The spares, tools and accessories' composition and positioning was altered.

At the same time, a number of improvements were introduced during overhaul, including double bakelitisation of the tanks and piping, enhancing the corrosion-resistant coating, restoration of parts' slots to their sizes, etc.

The upgrade resulted in a change in the IS-2's combat and technical characteristics, so the tank was designated as IS-2M. Mention should be made that the upgrade began in 1957 and ended in the mid-1960s. Hence, IS-2Ms often differed in modifications made and parts used depending on when they were overhauled. The whole IS-2 fleet operated by the Soviet Army was brought to IS-2M standard, after which there were virtually none left in the original configuration in the Soviet Union.

The Soviet Army had the IS-2M for a very long time, it having survived the younger IS-3 and IS-4. It was supposed to be finally replaced by the T-10, but the replacement was not completed. Following the deterioration of Soviet-Chinese relations in the 1970s, IS-2Ms and IS-3s equipped the fortified areas built along the Soviet-Chinese border in Transbaikalia and the Russian Far East. The tanks were situated in their parks and were to deploy to the border in their prepared firing points when put on alert. The last known exercise in which IS-2Ms participated was conducted in the Odessa Military District, and the Russian defence minister ordered the IS-2M to be withdrawn from service only in 1995!

An IS-2M in the Central Armed Forces Museum, Moscow, with smoke dischargers on its rear. Note the pipes from the fuel tanks to the engine.

Some IS-2s were reconstructed into IS-2T armoured recovery vehicles in the 1950s.

An IS-2 in the Warsaw Armour Museum.

This IS-2M has a welded-front hull made by Uralmashzavod in the Kubinka Armour History Museum.

An IS-2M in the
Central Armed
Forces Museum,
Moscow.

A cast casing of a
122-mm gun. The
Tsh-17 sight hole
is on the right.

The IS-2M during a military parade, Kubinka Armour History Museum, 2001.

An IS-2M converted into a monument in Moscow.

An IS-2 in the
Wojsko Polskie
Museum (Polish
National Military
Museum),
Warsaw.

IS-3

The development of a new heavy tank project, which would considerably surpass the mass-produced IS-2 in terms of armour protection, commenced in accordance with the 8 April 1944 resolution by the State Defence Committee although its genesis started earlier.

A group of researchers with the Stalin Military Academy of Mechanisation and Motorisation, led by A. Zavyalov, a colonel of the Corps of Engineers, examined the nature of the tanks' damage caused by artillery shells at the armoured battlefields near the Kursk battle. They found out that not all of the turret and hull sections were damaged identically. The front parts of the hull and the turret featured the higher damage probability, with the turret suffering the greatest number of hits.

The experimental Kirovets-1 tank (Object 703).

The design efforts saw stiff competition between two design teams – Experimental Plant 100 established in March 1942 and headed by Zh. Ya. Kotin and A. S. Yermolaev was striving to prove its leadership in heavy tank development, and the Kirovsky plant's design bureau led by N. L. Dukhov and M. F. Balzhy wanted to establish its maturity and independence.

The design proposed by the Kirovsky production plant featured an original flat turret designed by G. V. Kruchonykh. The turret was to mount the 122-mm D-25 gun. The very sloped armour of the turret made armour-piercing projectiles ricochet, and the good interior layout minimised its dimensions. This allowed the frontal armour to be increased to 255 mm compared to the IS-2's 100 mm without an excessive increase in the vehicle's weight.

Having learnt of the new tank under development by the Kirovsky plant in Chelyabinsk, Zh. Ya. Kotin was quick to come up with a design of his own, based on production plant's design experience obtained in developing Objects 244, 245 and 248. His tank version's unusual bow was noteworthy.

The upper glacis plate of both welded and cast hulls of all tanks of the time was a flat armour plate either vertical or slightly sloped from the vertical. Such a design was necessary as long as there were two crewmen at the front of the hull. With the radio operator/machinegunner becoming redundant and only the driver

remaining in the centre of the bow section, an opportunity appeared to cut the corners of the glacis plate. This is how the sloped sides appeared as part of the cast glacis plate of the IS-2. The design both ensured a reduction in the hull's weight and enhanced the strength of the armour when under frontal fire. Plant 100's designers G. N. Moskvin and V. I. Tarotko suggested that the whole glacis plate should be made with two plates joined at a peak and sloped sharply backward and to each side. Their open top was to be covered by a triangular roof slanted at 7 degrees from the horizontal. This roof was to have a hatch right above the tank driver, through which he could get into and out of the tank. Such a dual-slope bow was dubbed the 'hawk nose' by designers (however, another moniker, 'pike's nose', stuck).

The transition to the all-welded hull without large cast parts was due to the progress made by the welders led by Academician Ye. O. Paton, on the one hand, and that the foundry was operating at full capacity making cast turrets to fit IS-2 tanks, on the other.

On 28 October 1944, the Kirovsky plant's first tank prototype rolled out of the assembly shop and underwent a test ride. Oil leaking from the gearbox was spotted during the run, and the tank had to be returned to the workshop. In November, the vehicle underwent the 1,000-km factory trials and failed again. The designers and manufacturing engineers of the Kirovsky

The first operational IS-3 at Kirovsky Zavod, Chelyabinsk, 1945.

Rear view of the IS-3 with the antenna socket on the sloped turret side – an element characteristic of earlier versions.

plant realised that some of the modifications planned could hinder production and operation of the tank considerably. For this reason, they decided to abandon the 620-hp V-11 engine that overstrained the transmission, leave the design of the running gear, power unit and transmission the way they were, and limit themselves to beefing up the tank's armour protection only.

On 25 November 1944, the Kirovsky plant made the second prototype dubbed 'Example A' by the acceptance committee and Kirovets-1 by the plant. Soon, the vehicle was designated 'IS (Example 1) heavy tank' in line with the order of the commander of the Armoured and Mechanised Forces.

After the factory trials had been finished, the tank was sent to NIIBT's testing range for official tests held from 18 to 24 December. There it was examined by Marshal P. A. Rotmistrov, deputy commander of the Red Army's Armoured Corps. He walked around the vehicle, climbed into it, sat at the driver's combat station and, having listened to a detailed report by Programme Manager M. F. Balzhy, said: "This is the tank the Army needs!"

At the same time, Plant 100 and the TsNII-48 Central Research Institute unveiled their own project to upgrade the IS-2's armour protection. For this reason, TsNII-48's Moscow division carried out a comparative analysis of the two projects, with experts arriving at the following conclusion:

"Since each of the proposed designs has advantages of its own, the best solution to the problem of the IS-2's armour protection would be a design maximising the advantages of both designs offered. In particular, a new IS-2 armour protection design should include the following structural elements:

– the bow of the hull must rely on the dual-slope design from Plant 100s and TsNII-48;

– the hull's trough-shaped bottom from the Kirovsky plant should be used;

– the turret's design should embody the cupola-shaped cross-section concept from Plant 100 and the roughly elliptical longitudinal section concept from TsNII-48.

Preliminary calculations prove that the above solutions might result in the hull's armour protection falling within the weight limits, indicated by the Kirovsky plant and Plant 100, and ensuring only 34% probability of penetrating it by 88-mm projectiles at a muzzle velocity of 1,000 m/s. The probability that the hull designed by Plant 100 and TsNII-48 would be penetrated by the same ammunition was 39.5%. The penetration probability for the Kirovsky plant's hull equalled 44.1%.

Thus, two independent designs of the same tank were submitted to People's Commissar for Armour Industry V. A. Malyshev for approval. One design was introduced by the Kirovsky plant's Director I. M. Zaltsman and Chief Designer N. L. Dukhov and the other by Plant 100's Director/Chief Designer Zh. Ya. Kotin. After the designs had been reviewed and TcNII-48's recommendations taken into account, V. A. Malyshev issued Order 729 dated 16 December 1944, in which he set the procedure of the further development efforts. The vehicle was officially designated as Kirovets-1, a schedule was approved and a 10-vehicle pilot batch was ordered, with eight tanks to be made by 25 January 1945.

Thus the new 'breakthrough' tank emerged as a result of two design teams pooling their efforts that were indivisible. Before the Experimental Plant was established, most of its future designers had been on the staff of the Chelyabinsk-based Kirovsky plant, on which premises they had worked. Only later, were some of them assigned to the Experimental Plant. However, most of those reassigned remained at the main plant, carrying on with their design and production work at the Kirovsky plant.

The new vehicle was called Pobeda (Russian for 'victory') in the desk calendar of the Kirovsky plant's Director I. M. Zaltsman, In which he noted the progress being made. No matter how much he wanted to give 'his' tank an outstanding name, it entered full-rate production as IS-3 by tradition. The production plant did give it its in-house designation, Object 703 being used as the tank's ordinal number.

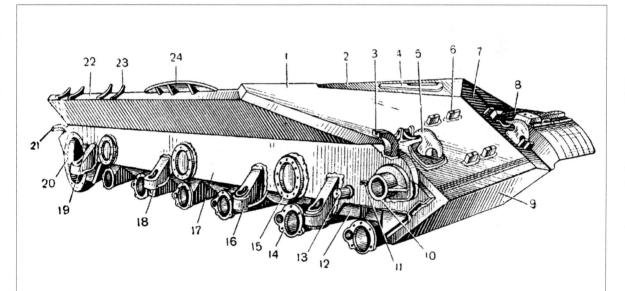

IS-3 hull:

1, 7 – sloped glacis plates;
2 – sloped front roof plate;
3, 21 – brackets for trackguards;
4 – driver's hatch cover;
5 – towing hook;
6 – spare track link attachment points;
8 – left-hand front mudguard;
9 – lower front plate;
10 – idler bell crank bracket;
11 – clamp;
12 – sloped side plate of hull bottom;
13 – trunnion;
14 – suspension unit;
15 – collar;
16 – suspension bump stop;
17 – vertical part of hull side;
18 – armoured torsion bar housing;
19 – attachment;
20 – opening for final drive;
22 – upper sloped hull side;
23 – additional fuel tank bracket;
24 – armour protection for turret overhang.

IS-3 was distinct
due to is peaked
glacis.

Turret rear and the roof of the engine compartment.

By 12 February 1945, two hulls of the IS-3 (Nos 2 and 3) had been assembled by the Kirovsky plant and sent to NIIBT's testing ground for firing tests. On 20 February, it was shown to the military acceptance committee and sent to Moscow. The firing range testing was conducted from 23 March to 11 April in Kubinka. Then the tank was shown to G. K. Zhukov and A. M. Vassilevsky. The two marshals reported to Stalin their impressions of the vehicle, and Stalin signed the resolution of the State Defence Committee on fielding the tank with the Red Army and its production by the Kirovsky plant. On 21 May, A. I. Blagonravov, chief of the Red Army's Technical Department of the Main Armoured Directorate, issued the order 'On Approval of the Technical Documents of the IS-3 Tank'. By 24 May, 29 IS-3s had been built, of which only 17 passed the factory testing.

The IS-3 heavy tank (Object 703) had a rather sophisticated hull and turret design with very thick armour plates. The halves of the glacis plate were set in the shape of a pike's nose and heavily slanted from the vertical. The top of the hull was reverse-slanted to house a wide turret ring. The sloping armour plates at the junction of its sides and bottom allowed a reduction in the overall hull surface area and an increase in armour protection owing to the weight reduction. The rear plate was made hinged for easier access to the power train.

The fuel-line connection of the exterior tanks.

71

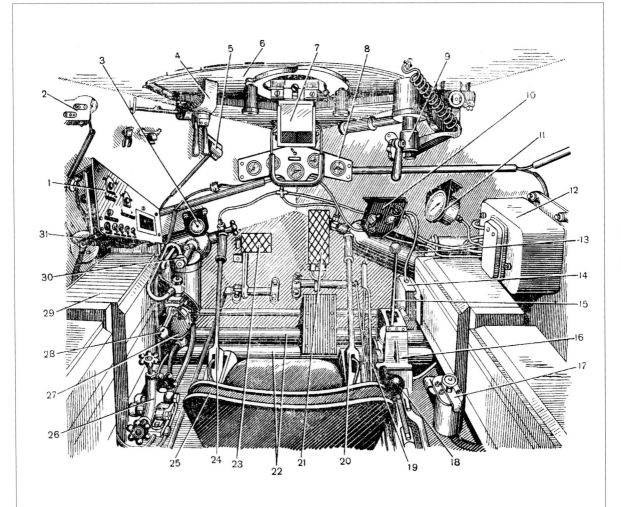

IS-3 driving compartment:

1 – driver's left instrument panel;
2 – driver's intercom headset connection;
3 – engine revolution indicator;
4 – hatch cover lock;
5 – panel lamp;
6 – driver's hatch cover;
7 – periscope;
8 – central instrument panel;
9 – hatch opening mechanism;
10 – compressed air starting control;
11 – speedometer;
12 – relay box;
13 – compressed air bottle;
14 – compressed air overflow tank;
15 – gear lever;

16 – gear lever gate;
17 – battery switch;
18 – manual fuel pump lever;
19 – auxiliary gearbox lever;
20, 24 – steering levers;
21 – accelerator;
22 – torsion bar springs;
23 – master clutch pedal;
25 – driver's seat;
26 – fuel distribution valve;
27 – auxiliary fuel pump;
28 – auxiliary fuel pump handle;
29 – batteries;
30 – priming fuel filter;
31 – intercom relay.

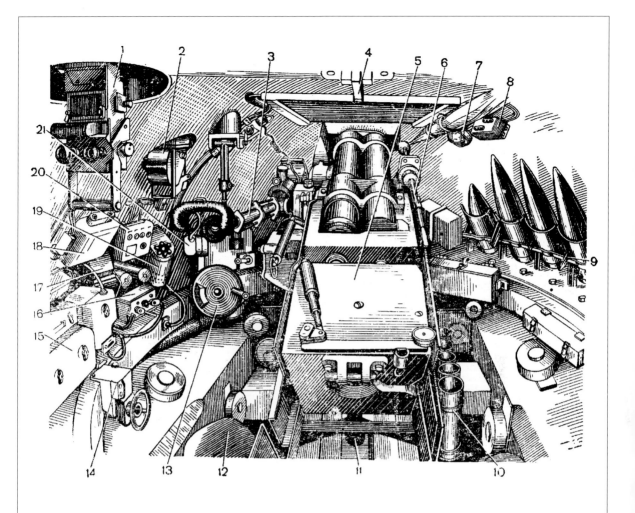

IS-3 fighting compartment:

1 – TPK-1 sight;
2 – gunner's periscope;
3 – TSh-17 sight;
4 – interior gun travel lock;
5 – gun;
6 – DTM machine gun;
7 – lamp cover;
8 – loader's intercom headset connection;
9 – ammunition stowage;
10 – stowage for five charge cases;
11 – turret rotating junction box;

12 – gunner's seat;
13 – handwheel of manual traverse gear;
14 – turret traverse lock;
15 – radio station;
16 – radio station power supply unit;
17 – antenna plug;
18 – commander's intercom headset connection;
19 – controller;
20 – turret electricity panel;
21 – turret traverse electric motor.

The turret hatch is closed by the double-leaf cover. The commander's cupola with the TPK-1 sight is the left leaf.

The driver sat in the front centre of the tank. There was a hatch with a side-opening cover fitted with an observation device. Before opening the hatch, the observation device had to be dismounted. There was an emergency exit hatch in the floor behind the driver's seat.

The cast turret had a flattened dome. There was a large oval hatch with two covers in the top of the turret. The loader's MK-4 observation device was in the right cover, while the commander's observation hatch was in the left one covered by a round rotating cap, in which the commander's observation device was installed. The device was designed for observing terrain, ranging and designating a target and controlling artillery fire. There was no prominent commander's cupola. Another MK-4 observation device was fitted to the upper-left part of the turret for the gunner.

The traversing mechanism was a planetary gear with manual and electric variable-ratio drives. The electric drive was equipped with the commander's control system. Keeping an eye on the target through his observation device, the commander could push a button on his device and traverse the turret in the right direction

through the shortest path. When the line of sight (LOS) matched the bore axis, the turret would stop. The turret's maximum traverse speed equalled 12 deg./s.

The 122-mm D-25T main gun dating back to 1943 and the 7.62-mm DT coaxial machinegun were mounted in a cast mantlet. The main gun was equipped with a two-chamber muzzle break and a horizontal sliding wedge with the mechanic semi-automatics. The armour-piercing projectile's muzzle velocity was 781 m/s. The aimed range of fire using the TSh-17 telescopic sight was 5,000 m. The actual max range extended to 15,000 m. The rate of fire was 2-3 rd/min.

There was a 12.7-mm DShK machinegun on the machinegun ring mounted on the roof of the turret.

The ammunition load totalled 28 separate loading rounds, including 18 HE/fragmentation and 10 armour-piercing (AP) rounds. Mention should be made that the AP ammunition stowage was painted black and the others iron-grey.

The ammunition load of the DT machinegun consisted of 945 rounds loaded in 15 magazines, while that of the DShK comprised five 50-round ammunition belts, with each belt stowed in a separate box. One box was mounted on the machine gun and the rest were kept in the fighting compartment.

The 12-cylinder V-11-IS-3 four-stroke liquid-cooled diesel V-engine, developing a maximum horsepower of 520 hp (382.5 kW) at 2,200 rpm and displacing 38,880 cc, was mounted on brackets welded to the sides of the hull.

The fuel system consisted of four internal metal box-like tanks with a total capacity of 450 litres mounted in parts as left and right groups beside the engine. Four external 90 litre cylindrical tanks were attached to the rear hull's sloping sides and connected to the internal tanks. The tanks were equipped with mechanical ejection devices consisting of cable-operated catches. The ejection handles were installed on the sides of the fighting compartment's rear.

The engine was started with a ST-700 electric starter or by compressed air from two 5-litre air bottles under the glacis plate. There was no inertia starter.

The power train was mechanical. The multiple-disk engine clutch was dry, steel-asbestos and bakelite. The eight-speed gear-box was man-ufactured with an auxiliary gear transmission. Two-storey planetary steering gears were installed on the ends of the gearbox main shaft. The planetary steering gear's locking friction clutches were a multiple-disk, dry, all-steel design. The brakes were a band, floating-type-cast-iron-to-steel design. The final drives were reduction gear sets with ordinary pinion and planetary rows.

There were detachable rims with 14 teeth on the track drive sprockets. The idler wheels were interoperable with the roadwheels. The track adjusting mechanism was a crank lever screw-type.

The tank was equipped with six pairs of roadwheels and three track return rollers on each side. The wheels' torsion-bar suspension was individual.

The track was made up of small links with cog-wheel engagement. The nominal number of links in each track was 86 and the minimum – 79. The links were connected with track pins. The link's pitch measured 160 mm and the width 650 mm. The link was a casting or a profile stamping.

The 24-volt electric equipment was single-wire. It was powered by a 1,500W electrostatic generator and four batteries.

IS-3s of the 71st Guards Heavy Tank Regiment on the Charlottenburg Highway, Berlin, 7 September, 1945.

IS-3s being
reviewed by
Allied generals.

The tank was equipped with a 10-RK-26 radio and TPU-4bisF intercom.

As mentioned above, the first batch of IS-3 tanks left the plant's workshops in late May 1945. They saw no action in the Great Patriotic War and the war against Japan.

These combat vehicles were unveiled to the international community in Berlin on 7 September 1945 during the Allied parade held to mark World War 2's end. The parade was reviewed by the commander-in-chief of the Soviet Occupation Forces, Marshal Georgy Zhukov, 3rd US Army Commander George Patton, British General Robertson and French General Koenig. Alongside, a large number of both Soviet and Allied top brass attended the event. The parade was opened by dismounted columns – Infantry from the 5th Soviet Shock Army's 9th Rifle Corps passed in review followed by the French 2nd Infantry Division, mountain infantrymen and Zouaves. The British 131st Infantry Brigade made a brilliant display. 1,000 paratroopers of the US 82nd Airborne Division closed the formation. After a short break, a mechanised column appeared, headed by 32 M24 General Chaffee light tanks and 16 M8 armoured cars of the US 705th Tank Battalion, followed by tanks and APCs of the French 1st Armoured Division. The British paraded 24 Comet tanks and 30 armoured cars of their 7th Armoured Division. Finally, 52 IS-3 tanks rolled along the Charlottenburg Highway. The Composite Tank Regiment was formed of the 71st Guards Heavy Tank Regiment, 2nd Guards Tank Army. The advanced design of Soviet tanks astonished the Allies.

In Moscow, the new tanks were showcased for the first time at a parade on 7 November 1946.

The IS-3 was in full-rate production until mid-1946, in conjunction with the IS-2 for a while in May 1945. The number of tanks built totalled 2,311. The per-unit cost was 350,000 roubles at the time. The tank entered service with the heavy armoured regiments of the Red Army. The only time these tanks saw action was in Hungary during the 1956 disturbances, with several vehicles being lost.

However, at the very beginning of the IS-3's service career, a whole range of deficiencies was revealed, resulting from errors dating back to the design stage. That is why an ad-hoc task force was set up as early as 1946 to analyse the failures of the IS-3's engine, gearbox, armoured hull elements in the engine compartment, etc. From 1948 to 1952, all the tanks were upgraded and modified under a modification programme. The engine-mounting brackets were reinforced, the gearbox holders were modified, the roof under the turret was strengthened, the engine clutch's design was improved and the seals of the final drives and roadwheels were improved.

First Moscow appearance of IS-3, 7 November, 1946.

Assigning missions at a tactical exercise, Leningrad Military District, 1947.

IS-3s were always welcome for Red Square parades from the late 1940s. Moscow, 1 May, 1947.

IS-3s during a military parade, Odessa, 7 November, 1948. In the late 1940s, victorious Marshal Georgy Zhukov commanded the Odessa Military District.

Armour in a tactical exercise, 1958.

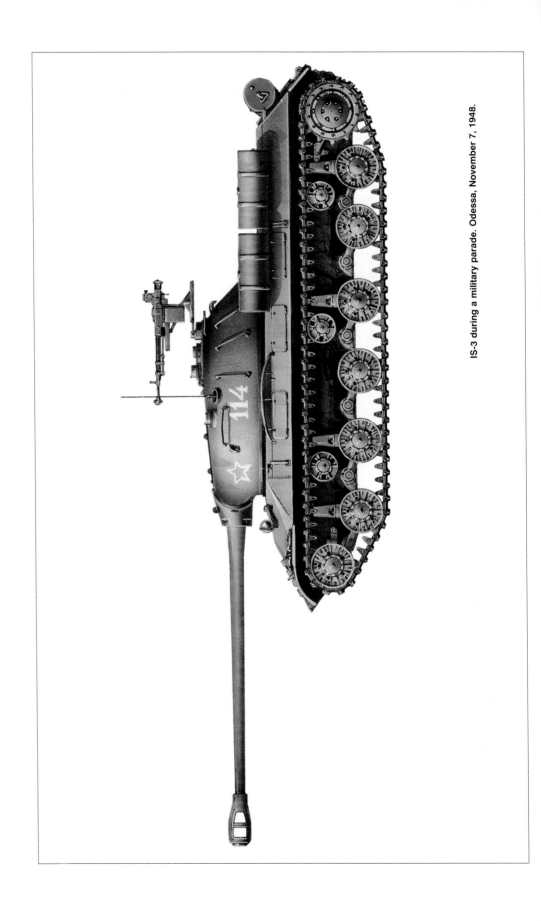

IS-3 during a military parade. Odessa, November 7, 1948.

The manual oil-booster pump was replaced with an electric one. The 10-RK radio was replaced by the 10-RT. The tank's weight increased to 48.8 tonnes.

In spite of the substantial and expensive modifications that cost a pretty penny (the design flaws elimination programme cost 260,000 roubles per tank), the vehicles failed to meet the operating requirements.

Late in the 1950s, the tank was modernised again, with the resulting variant being designated as IS-3M. The modernisation objective was to make the tank complete with other combat vehicles of the time and to maximise its commonality with more advanced tanks.

In the course of the upgrade, the following changes and additions were introduced:

– the structural rigidity of the hull was increased by the installation of bars in the rear plate and diagonal braces in the bottom; a hole was cut in the bottom under the gearbox and closed by an overlap-welded cover plate to increase the gap between the gearbox and the floor;

– the DShK machine gun was replaced by an upgraded DShKM and a DT machine gun with the DTM;

– the rotating plate on the commander's hatch was additionally sealed;

– the driver's TVN-2 night vision device was fitted;

– the V-11-IS-3 engine was replaced with the V-54K-IS developing a maximum of 520 hp at 2,000 rpm. The VTI-2 air purifier with two degrees of purification and pneumatic first-stage dust removal ousted the multicyclone-type air purifier. A new oil tank with a heat exchanger and a foam fire suppressor was fitted to the oil system. An electrically-driven heater was embedded in the cooling system. The hull's rear was provided with attachments to mount two 200-litre fuel barrels;

– the bearing mount assemblies of the road-wheels and idlers were reinforced and the gland seals were modified;

– an emergency lighting two-wire circuit was added to the electric equipment system. An electric outlet for slave starting was fixed in the rear. The commander's control system was removed from a number of tanks. The direct-acting instruments were replaced with electric gauges;

IS-3s in Red Square, Moscow, 1 May, 1960.

IS-3M

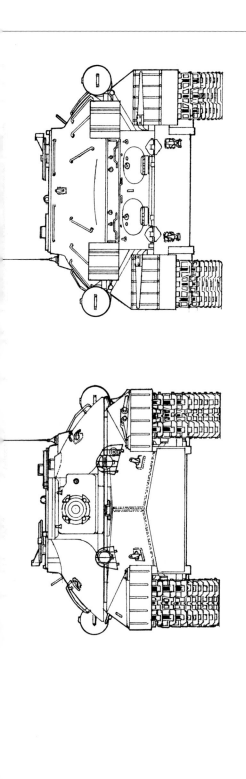

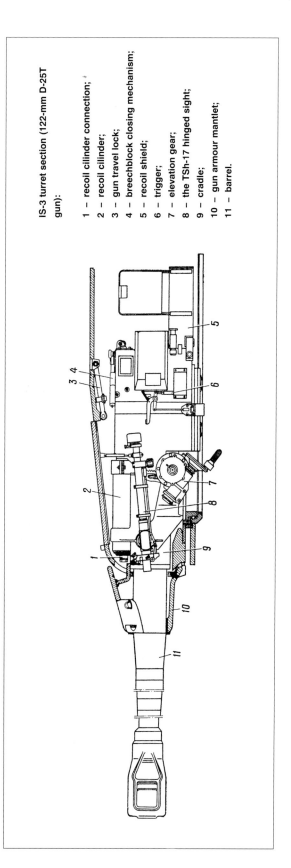

IS-3 turret section (122-mm D-25T gun):

1 – recoil cilinder connection;
2 – recoil cilinder;
3 – gun travel lock;
4 – breechblock closing mechanism;
5 – recoil shield;
6 – trigger;
7 – elevation gear;
8 – the TSh-17 hinged sight;
9 – cradle;
10 – gun armour mantlet;
11 – barrel.

– R-113 radio and R-120 intercom were installed.

Mention should be made that the upgrade greatly enhanced the tank's reliability. However, there was no future for the tank. The vehicles were dumped at tank parks and mothballed.

The IS-3's exports were virtually nil. In 1946, two tanks were given to Poland for design studies and instructor cadre training. Evidence suggests that the tank's introduction by the Polish Armed Forces was intended. In the 1950s, both vehicles participated in several military parades. Afterwards, one tank was used by the Military Technical Academy in Warsaw until the early 1970s and was used as a target at one of the gunnery ranges. The second tank lasted longer. It was given to the Officers' Armour School named after S. Czarnecki, in which museum it has been displayed ever since.

In the 1950s, one tank was given to Czechoslovakia for the same familiarisation and testing purposes.

A far greater number of tanks were sent to the Democratic People's Republic of Korea following the end of the Korean War. In the 1960s, two North Korean armoured divisions had a heavy-tank regiment each.

The Egyptian Army received its first IS-3s in the late 1950s. On 23 July 1956, they took part in the parade in Cairo on Independence Day. Most of the 100 IS-3s and IS-3Ms sold to Egypt were delivered between 1962 and 1967.

On 5 June 1967, the Israeli forces launched an offensive on the Sinai Peninsula, kicking off the Six-Day War. Mechanised forces and armour played the decisive role on the ground. The Israeli tank fleet was made up of US-made M48A2 tanks equipped with 90-mm guns, British Mk5 and Mk7 Centurions up-gunned with 105-mm main armament by Israel, and upgraded M4 Shermans carrying 105-mm main guns.

The Egyptians opposed the Israelis with Soviet-built T-34-85, T-54, T-55 and IS-3 tanks. IS-3s were in service with the 7th Infantry Division defending on the Khan Yunis-Rafah front. The 125th Armoured Brigade defending the El Kuntikulla area operated 60 IS-3s.

Soviet-made heavy tanks as well as other versions could have offered stiff opposition to the Israelis, but this did not happen, even though they damaged several M48s. On the fluid battlefield, the IS-3s gave ground to the more sophisticated Israeli tanks. This was due to their low rate of fire, small ammunition load and utterly outdated fire control system (M48A2s were fitted with optical sight/rangefinders and two-axis gun stabilisers). Moreover, the engines of the IS-3s were ill-suited for hot weather operation.

However, what mattered most was that the combat skills of the Egyptian crews were no match for those of their Israeli opposite numbers. The low general educational level of most of the Egyptian personnel was also among the reasons for the defeat, because it hampered their efforts to learn to operate the equipment. Morale was also low, as the Egyptian troops did not put up much of a fight.

The upgraded IS-3M.

The IS-3s of
Soviet Tank Force
in Germany were
the first to be
upgraded into the
IS-3M version.

The front and rear views of the IS-3M in the Minsk World War 2 Museum. The brackets on the rear are the same as those of the IS-2M.

IS-3M turret. An upgraded tank is recognisable from its conical antenna plug for the new R-113 radio station.

The antenna plug for the R-113 radio station and gunner's MK-4 sight.

The latter is well illustrated by a fact unusual in armoured combat, but typical for the Six-Day War. An IS-3M was damaged near Rafah by a hand grenade thrown into its open turret hatch. Egyptian tankers fought with open hatches so that they could quickly leave their tanks if they were hit. The retreating 125th Armoured Brigade's soldiers simply abandoned their tanks on the battlefield, with IS-3s among them. The Israelis captured them in perfect running order. As a result, the Egyptian Army lost 73 IS-3s and IS-3Ms. By 1973, there was only one tank regiment operating IS-3s. Nothing is known about its participation in the 1973 war.

The Israeli Army operated the captured IS-3Ms until the early 1970s. Their worn-out V-54K-IS engines were replaced with V-54 engines taken from captured T-54A tanks. At the same time, the roof of the engine compartment was borrowed from the T-54As as well. By 1973, when the next Arab-Israeli War broke out, most of the IS-3Ms were used as stationary firing units dug in along the Suez along the so-called Bar-Leva Line. They were irrelevant during the war and were re-captured by the Egyptians. This was the only significant example of the IS-3's tactical employment in battle.

The story of the IS-3 would be incomplete without mentioning the ISU-152 self-propelled gun designed in 1945 (Object 704) – an IS-3 derivative. The 120-mm-thick armour plate common for the front hull and the cabin was slanted heavily. The driver was placed in the cabin on the left and used the periscopic vision device mounted on the cabin's roof. The commander had all-round visibility by means of an MK-4 device on his rotating hatch door. The crew was five men strong.

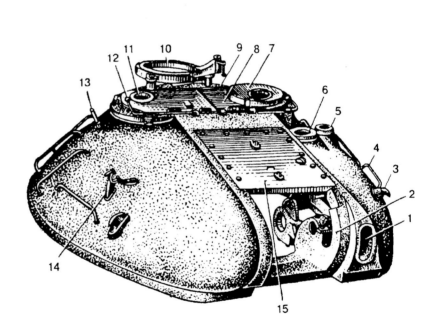

IS-3M turret:

1 – sight opening;
2 – slot for gun trunnions;
3 – lifting hook;
4 – hand-rails;
5 – antenna socket;
6 – gunner's periscope opening;
7 – rotating plate for commander's periscope;
8 – hatch cover;
9 – roof rear plate;
10 – ring mounting of the anti-aircraft machine gun;
11 – loader's periscope opening;
12 – hatch cover torsion bar;
13 – rod to stow the AA machine gun;
14 – clip to secure the AA machine gun's barrel when stowed;
15 – roof removable plate.

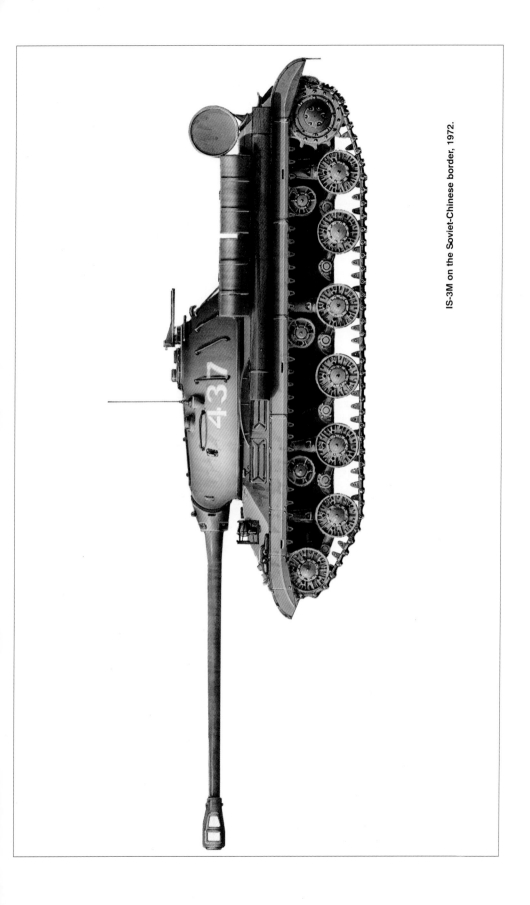

IS-3M on the Soviet-Chinese border, 1972.

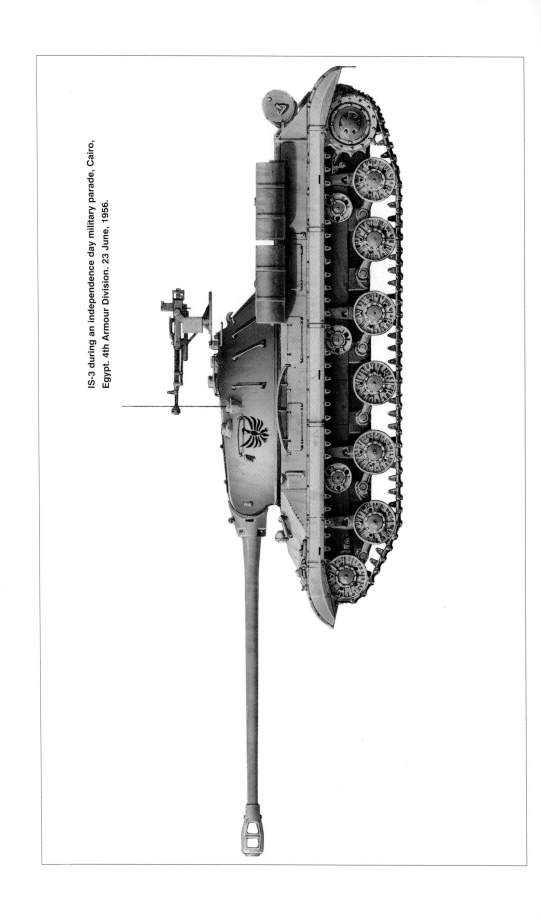

IS-3 during an independence day military parade, Cairo, Egypt. 4th Armour Division. 23 June, 1956.

An IS-3 captured by the Israeli forces in 1967 seen during a military parade. Tel-Aviv. Later most of the captured tanks were dug in on the bank of the Suez Canal.

Decommissioned IS-3s survived until the 1990s as targets at training sites.

Developed in 1944, the ML-20SM field gun-howitzer was fitted to a mantlet in the fighting compartment front armour. Its traverse angle was 11 degrees and elevation angle equalled +18 degrees, with its depression angle measuring 104 degrees. The ammunition load totalled 20 separate loading rounds. The TSh telescopic sight was used for direct fire and a panoramic sight for indirect. A special target designation system linked the commander, gunner and driver. A DShK heavy machinegun was coaxial to the main gun. A second DShK was mounted on the loader's hatch ring to engage hostile aircraft.

The 47.3-tonne vehicle powered by the 520-hp V-2IS engine could make 40 km/h, maximum. The fuel tanks' shape and capacity were modified too. The power train, running gear, electric equipment and communications gear were borrowed from the IS-3.

The SPG differed from other vehicles in its class chiefly by its good armour ensured by its heavily slanted armour plates and the unorthodox seating of the driver. However, the heavily slanted sides of the cabin, long recoil of the gun (up to 900 mm) and integration of the driver's and fighting compartments resulted in a considerable reduction in the fighting compartment's dimensions and hindered the crew's operation. Elevating the driver's seat reduced the angle of vision and hindered his operation due to high amplitude of oscillation. Only one vehicle of the type was made. It is displayed in the Armoured Materiel Museum in Kubinka.

As for the IS-3 tank, it outclassed its predecessor, the IS-2, in terms of performance. The IS-3 was highly appreciated abroad too. According to Dr. von Senger und Etterlin, a known West German expert, "the rational design of the bow and the turret is worth the highest appreciation. In addition, the tank has a rather low silhouette. In 1956, the IS-3 featured the best combination of combat characteristics among heavy tanks."

This may be so, but the design drawbacks affected its combat capabilities. In spite of two upgrades, the modifications were never a success.

The Object 704 self-propelled gun at the Kubinka Armour History Museum.

An IS-3M in the
museum of the
Far Eastern
Military District,
Khabarovsk.

IS-3M in Snegiri,
Moscow Region.

An IS-3M at the opening ceremony of the Omsk VTTV-2001 arms show.

An IS-3M during a military parade, Kubinka Armour History Museum, 2001.

An IS-3M in the
World War 2
Museum in
Moscow.

An IS-3 veteran tank leading a column of up-to-date battle tanks of the Russian Army during the Day of Tankman celebration at the Kubinka Armour History Museum on 10 September 2005.